# BARKING
## A HISTORY

To Brenda and John and family

Sue Curtis
2006

Aerial view of Barking in 1933. A Thames sailing barge moored at the Town Quay, on the River Roding, is visible in the bottom left corner.

# BARKING
## A HISTORY

*Sue Curtis*

# Phillimore

2006

Published by
PHILLIMORE & CO. LTD
Shopwyke Manor Barn, Chichester, West Sussex, England
www.phillimore.co.uk

ISBN 1 86077 224 2

Printed and bound in Great Britain by
CAMBRIDGE PRINTING

# Contents

# List of Illustrations

*Frontispiece*: Aerial view of Barking in 1933

# Acknowledgements

I would like to thank the late David Hilton, who died on 30 April 2002, for his help in the preparation of text for this book.

With regard to illustrations, I would particularly like to thank Judith Etherton (Archivist) at the London Borough of Barking and Dagenham. Aerofilms, *frontispiece*; Curtis Heritage Enterprises, xi, xii, 1, 4, 10, 13, 26, 29, 32, 34, 53, 56, 58-9, 76-80, 82-3, 85-6, 88, 92-3, 95-6, 98-104, 110, 113, 115, 118-20, 122-3, 125-6, 128-9, 131, 133-4, 136, 139-40, 143-5; *Dagenham Digest*, 108; Essex Archaeological Society, 11, Clapham, A.W. 'The Benedictine Abbey of Barking' in Transactions of the *Essex Archaeological Society*, xii, 2nd series, pp.69-87 (1912); London Borough of Barking & Dagenham, 2-3, 5-9, 15, 17-18, 20-8, 30-1, 33, 35-52, 54-5, 57, 60-75, 81, 84, 87, 89, 90-1, 94, 97, 105-9, 111-12, 114, 116-17, 121, 124, 127, 130, 132, 135, 137-8, 141-2, 146; Newham Museum Service, 12, 16, 19; *Victoria County History of Essex*, 14.

*This book is dedicated to my father,*
*the late John William Curtis (1924-2001),*
*who always supported and encouraged my writing career.*

# Introduction

Each working day I travel from home during the rush hour to my office located on the third floor of the Westbury Centre in Ripple Road, Barking. This building was formerly a school officially opened on 18 May 1904. I arrive from the east by electric train at the large, bustling station, a hub for main line and underground services in east London and south Essex. Stepping onto the platform, I make my way up the stairs towards the electronic ticket barriers and the vast concourse, with its huge concrete roof constructed in the early 1960s. It always feels like arriving at a major transport interchange, people dashing to and fro in the early morning stampede.

Immediately outside the busy terminus, taxis and buses queue to carry people along their way. School pupils and university students

East Street, Barking in the 1930s.

An elephant teaches children to cross the road safely at the junction of Station Parade and Ripple Road in the 1950s.

gather in clusters and gossip about yesterday's action and their plans for the day ahead while waiting for the red double-deckers travelling towards Dagenham, Ilford and Romford.

I leave this thronging scene behind, turning right, and walk down Station Parade towards East Street. I pass fast food outlets with transatlantic names such as 'Subway' and High Street banks such as Lloyds TSB on my way towards the pedestrian precinct and the controversial Bandstand, erected in recent years to provide a focal point in the main shopping area. As I pass by, a man of African descent often preaches Christianity and sings hymns, exhibiting great enthusiasm in all types of weather. On Wednesdays and Thursdays I call at a newsagents to purchase the latest edition of the local papers and catch up on the news.

At this point I turn left at Barclays Bank and head along Ripple Road. On market days this is a complex obstacle course of parts of stalls being set up and boxes of goods ready for sale. The scent of greasy fried onions and charred beef wafts from a burger stand. It is virtually impossible to visualise Blake's, Gay's or Garland's corners of the past.

I leave the pedestrian area and pass a new hanger-like Lidl store to my right. Keeping along Ripple Road I turn left towards the A13. I reach my workplace on foot within 15 minutes of leaving the railway station. The land the Westbury Centre occupies would once have formed part of the historic Westbury manor, part of the oldest and largest estate in the county of Essex.

During these short journeys I am always amazed how the rich and complex heritage of Barking town is virtually completely unseen and unknown in the midst of the modern development of this multi-cultural East London suburb. In this volume I aim to reflect upon the many past glories of the place which once housed the most important nunnery and ran the largest fishing fleet in England.

# One

# A TALE OF TWO RIVERS

The modern town of Barking forms half of the London Borough of Barking and Dagenham. This area is in the eastern reaches of England's capital city and the south-west of the county of Essex. It is a London suburb situated firmly in the commuter belt. From the earliest days of human settlement, however, the successful development of the town sprang from a highly strategic geographical location. Barking lies in close proximity to two rivers, the famous Thames and its smaller and lesser-known tributary, the Roding.

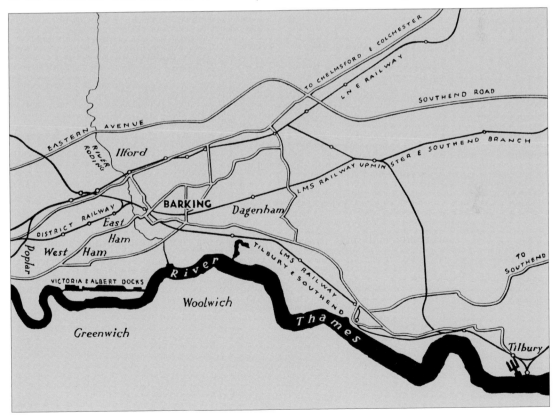

**1**  *Sketch map of Barking showing the rivers, roads and railways.*

1

The Thames is one of the world's great rivers. It started its life about 170 to 140 million years ago, during a period when much of southern England was still covered by sea. The waterway formed part of a much larger landmass that included Europe, North America and Greenland. At this time the river was a mere tributary of the mighty River Rhine on the continental landscape.

At the close of the Jurassic era, about 140 million years ago, the shells of various marine creatures were laid down to form the chalk landscape of the Thames valley. Each inch of chalk in the downs took about 2,500 years to create. When sea levels rose at the close of the last Ice Age, *c.*12,000 B.C., the North Sea rose over the Dogger Bank and Great Britain was separated from the mainland of Europe. The River Thames now flowed directly into the North Sea.

The Thames is tidal in nature between Teddington Lock and the estuary. Barking town developed on this tidal stretch, to the east of London, and throughout the town's history flooding has been a persistent problem. During the Middle Ages floods were frequent and serious, causing the temporary loss of large areas of pasture land. The heavy burden of maintaining the sea defences fell mainly on the abbess of Barking, who had to seek tax relief to pay for the works. Flooding was severe in 1377, 1382 and 1392 and on several occasions in the 15th century. By 1563 Barking came under the jurisdiction of a Court of Sewers, who dealt with Thameside areas from West Ham to Mucking; later the area came under the control of the Havering Levels. Further incidents were recorded in 1764, 1824, 1848 and 1888, when almost the whole of south-west Essex from Tilbury to Barking and Ilford was submerged. The last major incident involved freak weather conditions during 1953, when a severe storm at sea combined with a very high tide causing a massive tidal surge which killed 300 people, an event now known as 'The Great Tide'. Creekmouth was most seriously affected by the influx as most of the land is less than 10 feet above mean sea level. Water swept over the wharf wall during the early hours of the morning of Sunday 1 February. Fifty cottages belonging to the Lawes Chemical Company were flooded to a depth of between two and four feet. The police toured the flooded region waking up residents while Mr Stone, the nightwatchman at the Lawes factory, sounded the works siren to raise the alarm. River Road became an icy torrent, sweeping broken fencing and other debris along the way.

This scene was described in the *Barking and Ilford Advertiser*: 'Creekmouth families – many of them still in pyjamas – waded through downstairs rooms into the torrent that was River Road. Parents held children in their arms and stood knee deep in the icy water, wondering if the river wall would break. No transport could reach them.' Most of these people left to stay with friends and relatives nearby. Ambulances eventually transported evacuees up to Blake's Corner in the centre of the town. The landlord at the *Crooked Billet* public house at Creekmouth served tea and light refreshments to the outcasts in the public bar. On Monday afternoon the families returned to their homes to find their floors covered in about two inches of mud. Mr Bons, a storekeeper in the hamlet, lost much of his stock, washed away by the rushing flood waters.

Much investment has been ploughed in to improve the sea walls and river defences since this tragedy. The largest construction is the Thames Barrier, but there are also 36 smaller gates and barriers. The Thames Barrier is used approximately twice a year to deal with the

**2**  *The flooding of Highbridge Road, near the River Roding, in the early 20th century.*

North Sea surge tides which would result in flood damage affecting the huge population of England's capital city.

The shape and nature of the tidal Thames is in constant flux. During high tides the watercourse is wide and deep; at low tide the river is shallow, with only a narrow channel running down the centre. Today, natural habitats by the riverside in the Barking area have been replaced by artificial defences. Wildlife clings to the increasingly few areas of natural riverbank along the tidal part of the river.

The River Roding flows south from Molehill Green, to the east of Stanstead Airport, to join the Thames at Creekmouth in Barking. A nostalgic popular song with the title 'Barking Creek' composed in 1923 by Mr Joe Mott contains the refrain:

I'm going back to Barking Creek,
  The place where I was born,
I'm going back to Barking Creek,
  Where I left one sunny morn.
I long to see that dear old home,
  And waters flowing blue,
I'm going back to Barking Creek but it will be
  A long time before I do.

Ironically, Barking Creek and its environs lost much of their distinctive maritime character in the 1920s when many associated buildings were

demolished. Mr Mott may not have recognised his dear old home! In 1922 the water mill was taken down and a few years later the housing on the edge of the Town Quay disappeared. The Roding valley is low-lying land with no notable hills. The lower reaches of the Roding valley have also always been prone to flooding. The area is composed of London clay and difficulties have historically been encountered after periods of heavy rain and melting snow, as natural drainage is very poor. On the eastern bank of the river mouth a small and isolated hamlet developed at Creekmouth. Owing to its remote location, magazines used for gunpowder storage were built here in 1719. Over 100 tons of dangerous materials were stored, so no housing or industrial works were constructed nearby.

This lasted until 1857 when Lawes Chemical Company began manufacturing artificial fertilisers on the site. They also built housing at Creekmouth for their workers. This developed into Creekmouth village, with a mission church and a public house named the *Crooked Billet*. In 1878 there was a major tragedy in the Thames off Barking Reach. A pleasure vessel called the *Princess Alice* sank and over 800 passengers were drowned. The villagers at

**3**   *The* Crooked Billet *public house at Creekmouth, depicted in 1904 by A.G. Stout.*

Creekmouth, who were enjoying a fair, heard the cries of the people in the water and tried their best to help. However, the end result was the setting up of a temporary mortuary in the hamlet.

The passenger steamer *Batavier* also sank in Barking Reach on 19 October 1872, and two lives were lost. The vessel had left Blackwall shortly after lunch to head for Rotterdam, and then for the Rhine. It collided with the *Charkee*, a large Turkish man-of-war, near the pumping station of the Southern Outfall Sewer. Most of the passengers and crew of the two vessels were safely rescued but, in the confusion, a child sleeping in a cabin of the *Batavier* was overlooked, and a boy crew member also drowned.

The new environmental phenomenon of global warming makes it an increasing likelihood that disastrous flooding may recur

in the next half century or so. This is further complicated by the mass construction of new housing by the river on former marshland, such as the Barking Reach complex. In order to protect urban land in the lower reaches of the Roding, the Barking Flood Barrier now guards the mouth of the river. Further north, towards the Town Quay, is the Barking Barrage, which was constructed in 1999. This structure now holds water in the Mill Pool when the tide ebbs. It aims to create an improved view of the riverside near Barking town centre, and to help stimulate economic regeneration in the Roding valley. In the future it may even be possible to visualise a marina developing in the Mill Pool area.

In the past the Mill Pool was an area of traditional industry. As the name suggests, a watermill developed which was associated with Barking Abbey. The local lord of the

**4**   *The Town Quay in 1832, by W. Bartlett.*

**5**   *Artificial defences at the Town Quay, c.1960.*

manor, formerly the abbess of Barking, had the right to provide milling facilities. All the corn grown on the manor of Barking could be ground only at this mill, and the lord charged a toll for this service. In the year 1321-2 the income from this activity appears to have been £19 16s. 11½d.

A manorial farming account for the period sets down the detailed costs of extensive repair work to Barking Mill. Fifty wooden lathes used to repair the walls of the Mill House cost 3½d.; the charge for fixing and plastering this material was 6d. The workings of the watermills were restored using iron (costing 18s. 10d.) and wood for timber piling (costing £1 10s. 1d.) Extensive work to the wharves, floodgates and sluices was carried out.

In the reign of King Henry VIII Barking Mill was valued at £20 per annum. The secular lords of the manor who took charge after the dissolution were not so keen to carry out the regular, expensive maintenance work. In the 17th century both Sir Thomas Fanshawe and his grandson of the same name were presented at the Quarter Sessions for failing to undertake essential repair works.

Navigation from Barking Mill north up to Ilford Bridge was improved with the adoption of the Roding Navigation Act of 1737. In the early 18th century the Smith family of millers sold the lease of Barking Mill to Mr Whitbourne of Leatherhead. In the 1850s Francis Whitbourne invested £8,000 in the mill, installing steam power. In 1862 T.D. Ridley and Sons purchased the enterprise and used both steam and water power at the mill, but later moved to Chelmsford and all the plant was offered for sale in 1905.

This was the beginning of the end of milling at the Town Quay and the Mill House. Mill and connecting bridge were all demolished in 1922. All that is left of the industry is a red-brick and slate-roofed Granary, constructed in 1870, which was used as a warehouse. This now houses a greetings card factory, but still provides a focal point.

**6**  *Barking watermill, c.1860.*

There were also windmills on waterside sites in Barking. Chapman and André's map of 1777 shows one behind the site of the current *Fishing Smack* public house on the banks of the Roding. It is believed to have been built in the early 18th century. More recently, Wellington Mill was constructed in the year of Waterloo, 1815, and Mr Whitbourne of Loxford Hall purchased the lease of the building in the following year. This was a weather-boarded smock-mill with four sails and four pairs of grinding stones. In 1905 the mill lost two sails in a gale and the others were removed. It was converted to electric power in 1906 but wheat growing in Essex was declining by this time. The building was unfortunately demolished in 1926, but a circular stone about two feet in diameter and inscribed 'Wellington Mill 1815' is in the collection of artefacts housed at Valence House Museum in Dagenham.

When Barking Abbey was founded, during the Saxon era, a wharf must have existed as waterways were the main means of transportation. All the major local industries, from traditional

**7** *The Georgian Mill House, seen clearly next to the Granary, was demolished in 1922.*

**8** *The Granary at Barking Town Quay.*

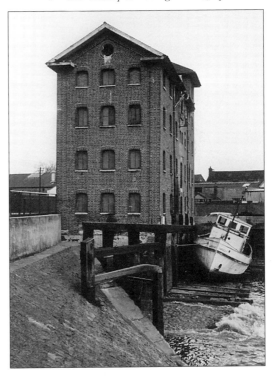

**9** *Barking Creek, depicted by W.L. Wyllie.*

milling and tanning to modern day chemical manufacture, have relied on the wharf. When the manor of Barking was purchased by Sir Thomas Fanshawe, in 1628, the Town Quay formed part of the property. By 1684, however, the Quarter Sessions were putting the responsibility for the Town Quay's upkeep onto Barking parish. In 1714 the Vestry decided to charge everyone using it. A turnpike was erected to facilitate the collection of tolls.

The changes to the character of the Town Quay area in recent years will have a far-reaching environmental significance. Mud flats, which provided a valuable habitat for wildlife, now lie permanently submerged. New mud flats have been created to the south of the Barking Barrage, in an attempt to compensate for this loss, but the long-term environmental effects of this new feature cannot be assessed in 2006. It will be many years before the results of environmental monitoring are clear. In recent times the River Roding has suffered from some incidents of water pollution. In 1985, for example, a pesticide entered the river via the Brookhouse Brook, a tributary joining the Roding at Abridge, but the area has now recovered thanks to effective environmental management.

There are exciting plans for urban and economic regeneration for Barking. For the last ten years, work has been taking place to promote an area known as 'The Thames Gateway'. Barking lies at the heart of this scheme and has seen major initiatives such as 'Barking Reach', where the Great Fleete housing development is now being occupied.

The Thames Gateway London Partnership is currently Europe's largest regeneration initiative. It covers areas on both sides of the Thames from Tower Bridge to Thurrock and Dartford with Barking in the very centre of the proposed development area. Barking and Dagenham Council is one of the partners involved in this initiative to provide new job opportunities, homes and environmental improvements. The organisation has published on the internet an ambitious vision for areas to the east of London by the year 2006, and dramatic changes should begin to appear soon, such as the redevelopment of Freshwater Estate in the Roding valley. East London will be changed significantly in the next few years in the build-up to the Olympic Games, 2012.

# Two

# EARLY SETTLEMENT

From prehistoric times right up to the present day, the Roding Valley has been suitable for settlement and development. This has resulted in the rich cultural, maritime and industrial history of Barking and district.

The oldest evidence of a person living in Britain was found on the south bank of the River Thames. It is the skull of a woman who lived about a quarter of a million years ago. It is believed that people settled in the Thames valley while Britain was still connected to mainland Europe, before the start of the last Ice Age. As the weather became colder the settlers retraced their steps and moved back to the east. Old photographs record evidence of arctic weather in relatively recent times. In 1895, Barking Creek on the River Roding was completely frozen over and ice skating became a popular local pastime.

The climate warmed again after around 10,000 B.C. and river valleys, such as the Thames, became suitable for human settlement. Britain had separated from Europe around 12,000 B.C. These Stone-Age people developed improved techniques for making flint tools and ceramics, and Stone-Age hand-axes and other flint implements were discovered in Ripple Road and near Barking Creek. In the New Stone Age, settlers in the Thames Valley region began to clear forested areas and plant crops. This was the beginning of agriculture in the Barking area. Market gardening was still a major source of income for local landowners in the late Victorian period, when the Glenny family were involved in producing vegetables for the Covent Garden market in London.

The early Bronze Age started around 2,000 B.C., when settlers from Spain, the Beaker People, sailed into the Thames estuary. They had metalworking and trading skills. Bronze-Age artefacts have been found in nearby Dagenham and a wooden figure popularly known as the 'Dagenham Idol', London's earliest representation of a human figure, was excavated from the marshy site of the giant Ford Motor Works in the 1920s. Celtic people crossed the Channel from c.500 B.C. They enjoyed the advantage of new iron weapons and tools, but the structure of ancient Britain was still predominantly tribal at this time. In the last century before Christ, the Belgic tribes invaded from the continent. The Catuvellauni settled on the north bank of the Thames and conquered the Trinovantes in what is present-day Essex. This allowed them to control the north bank of the Thames estuary.

It was, however, Roman invaders who saw the cultural and strategic significance of the

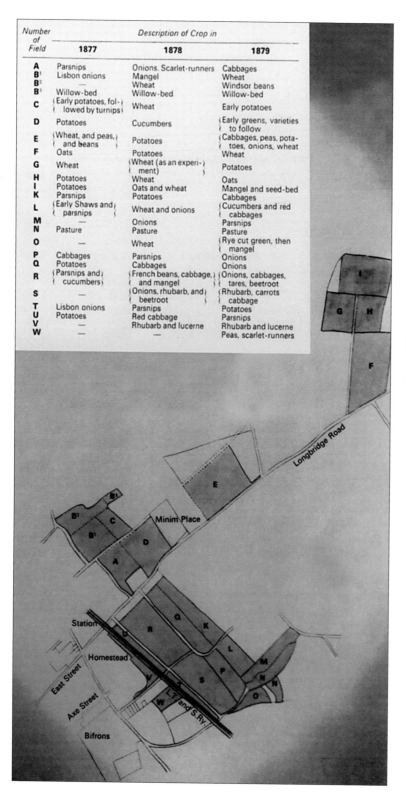

| Number of Field | Description of Crop in | | |
|---|---|---|---|
| | 1877 | 1878 | 1879 |
| A | Parsnips | Onions. Scarlet-runners | Cabbages |
| B¹ | Lisbon onions | Mangel | Wheat |
| B² | — | Wheat | Windsor beans |
| B¹ | Willow-bed | Willow-bed | Willow-bed |
| C | Early potatoes, followed by turnips | Wheat | Early potatoes |
| D | Potatoes | Cucumbers | Early greens, varieties to follow |
| E | Wheat, and peas, and beans | Potatoes | Cabbages, peas, potatoes, onions, wheat |
| F | Oats | Potatoes | Wheat |
| G | Wheat | Wheat (as an experiment) | Potatoes |
| H | Potatoes | Wheat | Oats |
| I | Potatoes | Oats and wheat | Mangel and seed-bed |
| K | Parsnips | Potatoes | Cabbages |
| L | Early Shaws and parsnips | Wheat and onions | Cucumbers and red cabbages |
| M | — | Onions | Parsnips |
| N | Pasture | Pasture | Pasture |
| O | — | Wheat | Rye cut green, then mangel |
| P | Cabbages | Parsnips | Onions |
| Q | Potatoes | Cabbages | Onions |
| R | Parsnips and cucumbers | French beans, cabbage, and mangel | Onions, cabbages, tares, beetroot |
| S | — | Onions, rhubarb, and beetroot | Rhubarb, carrots cabbage |
| T | Lisbon onions | Parsnips | Potatoes |
| U | Potatoes | Red cabbage | Parsnips |
| V | — | Rhubarb and lucerne | Rhubarb and lucerne |
| W | — | — | Peas, scarlet-runners |

**10** *Plan of Mr W. Glenny's market gardening enterprise on Longbridge Road, showing the crop rotations from 1877 to 1879.*

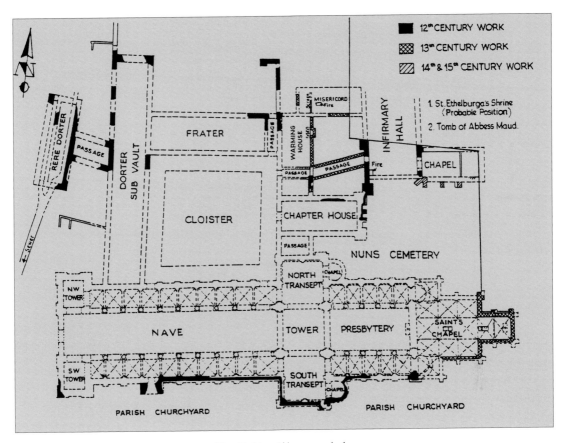

**11**  *Barking Abbey ground plan.*

waterway they called 'Tamesis'. In the earliest expedition to Britain, in 55 B.C., troops were commanded by Julius Caesar. By the first century A.D. they were under the influence of Emperor Claudius. The main road the Romans built connecting the major settlements of London and Colchester passed through Chadwell Heath, near Barking. It is believed that Roman bricks and tiles were later utilised in the construction of Barking Abbey. The Anglo-Saxons stood in awe of the sophisticated Roman building works, but this did not prevent them from using a handy local source of materials! Roman pottery and a coin of Magnentius have been discovered during excavations on the abbey site. There is other evidence of the Roman occupation. In 1932 a

stone coffin plus shards of third-century pottery were discovered in Ripple Road. More ceramics and a Roman brooch were found in Westrow Drive as new private houses were being built. Further Roman finds came to light during the construction of the Becontree Housing Estate in the 1920s and 1930s.

The profound influence of the imperial Romans began to decline in the mid-fourth century. The Saxons from North Germany and Denmark first invaded England in *c*.A.D. 367. The Romans left England in 411 and the Saxon raids intensified. The newcomers gradually settled in England, establishing small hamlets all along the River Thames. They came with distinct traditions of house construction,

technology and burial, all of which were different from the established Romano-British customs and practices. Barking and neighbouring Dagenham were amongst the earliest Saxon settlements in the Essex area. It is believed that Barking was known as 'Berecingum', literally 'Berica's people', named after a local tribal chieftain. At first people lived in extended family groups, possibly reflecting the culture of their homelands, but leaders of the dominant tribes, in a system of survival of the fittest, developed small kingdoms.

Other areas nearby have been important sources of Saxon finds. At Rainham, once known as 'Roeningham' (settlement of the ruling people), gravel diggers discovered a significant collection of artefacts in 1937. The rich hoard included a rare glass drinking horn, small wooden buckets, shield bosses, rings, brooches, spearheads and swords.

Pope Gregory sent St Augustine to England to convert the country to Christianity in 597. In the space of a few generations the pagan gods were fully replaced by Christian beliefs. In less than a century this new movement had led to the founding of the great Thames-side monasteries, such as the one at Barking. The town became the site of one of the most important, as well as one of the earliest, abbeys in the country. It existed for nearly 900 years and had a massive impact on the area.

# Three

## A GREAT FOUNDATION

One of the major events in the history of Barking took place in A.D. 666, when Erkenwald, who later became Bishop of London, founded Barking Abbey for his sister Ethelburga and Chertsey Abbey for himself. Both were pioneers in re-establishing Christianity in this part of the country and Barking Abbey began a mere 13 years after Christianity was re-established in Essex. Both were believed to be descendants of the royal families of East Anglia, Mercia and Surrey. Ethelburga was the first abbess in charge of the foundation, and a nun called Hidilitha had to come over the English Channel from an abbey at Faremoutier en Brie in Normandy to tutor her for this new responsibility.

It is likely that pagan Barking had been a site of regional significance long before the Saxon era and could have acted as a centre for pagan rites. The area also linked easily to other religious beacons via Green Lane. The development of Christian practices on this significant site would help to explain how one of the most important nunneries in England came to be built in the middle of a flood plain.

The practice of Christianity had ebbed and flowed in south-east England since its original introduction by the Romans. Even after the missions of St Cedd, who founded a monastery at Tilbury in Essex, there was a brief, partial relapse into pagan practices. Erkenwald's influence, however, led to a decline in Celtic foundations such as Tilbury and the growth of the more communal type of monastery such as Barking.

There was no deed of foundation in 666, although a later document dated 692-3 confirms the official grants of land, possibly given verbally when the abbey was a new institution. This Anglo-Saxon manuscript is commonly known as 'Hodilred's Charter' (or Ethelred's Charter) and it now forms part of the Cotton Collection at the British Museum.

**13**  *The coat-of-arms of Barking Abbey.*

13

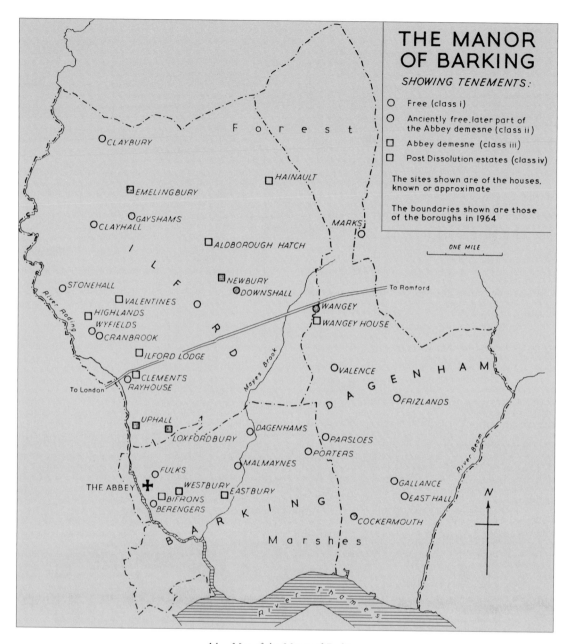

**14** *Map of the Manor of Barking.*

It is the second oldest Anglo-Saxon charter in existence. Signatories included Sebbi, King of the East Saxons, who jointly ruled the area with his nephew Sighere. The land signed over to Barking Abbey eventually became the oldest and largest estate in Essex, and was known as the Manor of Barking. It included the whole of present-day Barking, Dagenham and Ilford.

The Saxon abbey, dedicated to St Mary, was a double house for men and women, who were physically separated by a wall, as at Whitby in Yorkshire. The abbess managed the institution and all the inhabitants. Such foundations were typical in England and northern France in the pioneering days of Christianity. The male inhabitants were monks who could celebrate mass and administer the sacrament, both acts forbidden to the nuns. In remote and wild areas the monks even acted as bodyguards to the women.

Erkenwald was made the fourth Bishop of the East Saxons, and he died on 30 April 693 whilst visiting his sister at Barking. In spite of protests from the nuns, his body was removed and transported to the capital city. He was buried in St Paul's, London, and had a shrine in the cathedral. He was canonised, as was Ethelburga who is believed to have died soon after her brother. Erkenwald had a marked Romanising influence upon the See of London, and the effects of this continued

for centuries after his death. In his *History*, the Venerable Bede tells of many miracles associated with the early days of Barking Abbey. The holy women Hildilitha, Edith and Tortgyth, as well as the child Esica, were all made saints. Their feast days were religiously marked at the abbey until the dissolution.

The site of the first Barking Abbey has been a matter of dispute. Ernest Loftus published his thesis in 1954, and local historian Herbert Hope Lockwood published his theories in 1986 in 'Where was the first Barking Abbey?' In recent years, however, the excavation of large amounts of Saxon material to the immediate west of the medieval ruins, by Newham Museum Service and other archaeological organisations, suggests that it existed on the same spot for all 1,400 years of its existence. The jury is still out on this topic, though, and it is likely that further

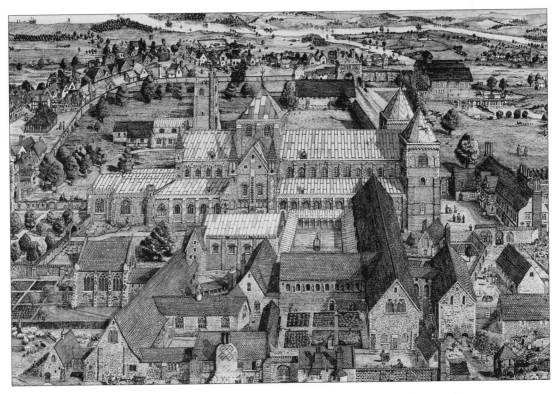

**15** *Reconstruction of how Barking Abbey may have appeared c.1500 by A.C. Rolfe.*

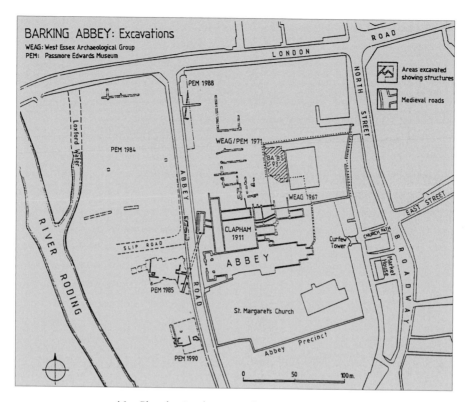

**16** *Plan showing the extent of recent excavation work.*

**17** *The ruins of Barking Abbey and the old Church of England School, c.1967.*

**18** *Medieval floor tiles, possibly from Barking Abbey, now in the possession of St Margaret's Church.*

**19** *Excavation of the main drain of Barking Abbey by Passmore Edwards Museum, Newham in 1985.*

research and excavation will be required in order to make a final decision.

Archaeological evidence does illustrate the rich quality of life in the Saxon abbey. Ceramics were imported from continental Europe, sophisticated glass vessels were used, and gold thread was woven into the lavish garments worn by the nuns. In a treatise on virginity, St Aldhelm complained about the style of wearing gold thread in their costumes recently adopted by religious women. At Barking the threads were formed of finely twisted, thin strips of pure gold. The women here were obviously very influential, rich and powerful, and their preferred clothing was a visual manifestation of the fact.

From 720 through to 870 there are no records for Barking Abbey. England was in the historic era known as the 'Dark Ages' and experiencing invasions from the sea by people we now know as Vikings. These pagans destroyed all the abbeys in their path. The 'Danish' invasion eventually resulted in England having a Scandinavian ruler, King Canute (or Knut in his native tongue). According to the 'Nova Legenda', the Saxon Abbey at Barking was destroyed by invading Vikings and the nuns were 'put to death by the Danish pagans'. After 886 Barking fell within the geographical area settled by the Vikings, traditionally known as 'Dane Law'. During this period Christian activities would not have been allowed to continue on the abbey site, although life carried on for people living in the Barking district. We know the nordic invaders influenced the local population significantly, as similarities occur between small metal finds from Saxon deposits and artefacts discovered at Danish Viking sites of this period.

After the death of King Alfred, the reconquest of the Dane Law began. Barking Abbey could function once more as a Christian establishment after Edward the Elder finally expelled the Danes from west Essex. From about the mid-10th century, it became a medieval nunnery. The old custom of housing monks and

nuns in the same institution was not morally acceptable to the Roman Church. Property was recorded as being bequeathed to the medieval institution in 951. The first abbess in the restored abbey was called Wulfhilda. She was of noble birth and was appointed by King Edgar the Peaceable, who had attempted to court her when she was about twenty years old.

Barking became a Benedictine abbey following reforms by Archbishop Dunstan, and was rededicated to St Mary and St Ethelburga. After 975, when Edgar died, Wulfhilda was evicted from Barking by his widow, Elfrida, and sent to a small monastery at Horton. Her exile ended in 993, and Wulfhilda returned to Barking Abbey for the final seven years of her life. Her relics were kept in the same feretory as those of St Ethelburga and St Hildilitha, and she was commemorated in the abbey services along with them. From this time, daily life at the abbey was regulated by the Benedictine rule of prayer, study and work. The Ordinale sets out the liturgical calendar and provides for all ceremonial activities. The liturgy of the Divine Office took precedence over all other affairs such as attending to the poor and caring for the sick.

**20** *(left)   The Seal of Surrender for Barking Abbey.*

**21** *(Below)   Brooch found during the Clapham excavation of 1910.*

**22** *The North Gate of Barking Abbey.*

**23** *The North Gate of Barking Abbey as it would have appeared in 1800, from a watercolour by A.B. Bamford.*

**24**    *The Gateway, Barking Abbey, in a publication of 1818. This shows the Curfew Tower in the early 19th century.*

**25** *The shaft of a Saxon cross displayed in St Margaret's Church.*

Benedictines followed an extremely rigid daily routine which provided a balance between prayer, study and work. Each day the nuns were expected to attend seven services, rising at two in the morning for Matins, followed by the second service known as Lauds. After this they returned to bed for three more hours' welcome sleep before rising at six to attend the Prime service. The Tierce, Sext, None Vespers and Compline services followed, finishing at eight in the evening when the nuns could retire to bed. Labour took place between one and six in the afternoon when nuns spent their time haymaking or digging. The majority of the day was spent in silence, or using a sign language to communicate, speech being allowed only during certain relaxation breaks. The diet was fairly healthy, as the nuns had a good supply and choice of produce from the farms situated on the manor of Barking lands. Regular helpings of bread, meat, beer, vegetables and dairy produce were available locally. In addition, the abbey purchased large supplies of salt, spices and fish to add taste and variety to the meals.

In the next century, there was to be radical change after the Normans invaded England. Barking Abbey was an extremely resilient institution, however, and proved to be the only early Saxon monastic foundation to survive until the dissolution in 1539. A physical reminder of the Saxon abbey now forms part of a collection of artefacts at St Margaret's parish church in Barking Broadway. Part of the shaft of an ornate, carved stone cross dating from the late 10th century was rediscovered in 1911, following re-use in the construction of one of the walls in the churchyard.

Examples of late Saxon works of art are rare survivals in Greater London and the fragment of stone from Barking Abbey is a most unusual find. Different abstract patterns are cut into each of the four sides of the shaft. These designs resemble the intricate curved designs seen in the wonderful illuminated manuscripts of this period.

## *Four*

# MEDIEVAL REALMS

The Norman invasion of England took place in 1066 and Harold, the Saxon king, was killed in the Battle of Hastings. On Christmas Day William the Conqueror was crowned King of England at Westminster Abbey. As the service proceeded, there was fighting on the streets outside.

Following the coronation, William withdrew immediately to Barking to consider his next move. He gave instructions for a fort to be built on Tower Hill in London, on land belonging to Barking Abbey, and established his headquarters at Barking during the construction period. In Barking, and at Berkhamsted, the

**26** *William the Conqueror at Barking, in a scene from the Charter Pageant of 1931.*

23

King began to receive the submission of Saxon earls and nobles. The initial surrender took place at Barking in January 1067, when prominent northern earls such as Edwin of Mercia and his brother Morcar of Northumbria arrived to pay homage to their new lord and master. During his stay in Barking the new King was likely to have made use of the ancient earthworks at Uphall, to the north of the abbey, in addition to the monastic buildings. His temporary base was very convenient both for the highway into his capital city and for routes to the sea or inland via the River Thames.

The abbess at Barking during this period was called Aelfgiva. She hosted the surrender of land to the abbey, thereby gaining royal favour, and from this time the abbey became known as the most important nunnery in the country and enjoyed close links with royalty. A mutilated stone slab, preserved in the wall of St Margaret's Church, commemorates Abbess Aelfgiva and Maurice, Bishop of London. In 1086, the widespread holdings of the abbey were listed in the famous Domesday Book. This survey revealed that in addition to the manor of Barking, property and land were owned in Great Warley, Stifford, Mucking, Bulphan, North Benfleet, Great Wigborough, Ingatestone, Hockley and Tollesbury in Essex. There were also 28 houses and half of the church of All Hallows-by-the-Tower in London, as well as lands in Surrey, the manor of Tyburn in Middlesex, the manor of Slapton in Buckinghamshire and the manor of Liddlington in Bedfordshire. Dagenham does not appear as a separate entity.

King William never visited Barking again and he died in 1087, following a fall from his horse in battle. He had, however, started the important tradition of royal patronage that led to Barking Abbey developing as an extremely rich and powerful institution. The abbesses were all selected from the ruling class, and were significant women in England. The abbess of Barking enjoyed precedence over all the other abbesses in England. Her status was that of a baron, a member of the medieval nobility. The King often used his position to appoint a close relative to this privileged position. The head of the abbey was supported by a prioress, who assisted in governing the foundation and deputised in the absence of the abbess. Under her were a sub-prioress, a high cellaress, an under-cellaress, a chamberlain, a kitchener, and two treytoresses who ran the refectory. The chantress organised church services and rehearsed singing. The sacrist arranged for the abbey church to be cleaned and decorated for religious festivals. The almoner attended to the poor people and the firmaress cared for the sick, including the poor patients suffering from leprosy. Inhabitants included small children, schoolgirls, novices, nuns, chaplains, corrodians, officers and servants. There was a private school for the novices, who came from the nobility and the official class.

The first regal abbess was Queen Maud, wife of King Henry I. She paid for the construction of a new road and two bridges with connecting causeway across the River Lea, south of the old crossing at Stratford. The first official post-Conquest abbess was Agnes, who died in 1136. King Stephen then appointed his wife Queen Mathilda (also known as Maud) as abbess. He gave the abbey in fee-farm for an annual rent of £16, making the offering himself before the altar. He later appointed to run the abbey Adelicia, who founded a leper hospital at Ilford. Many institutions of this type were founded in the 12th century to care for people suffering from the incurable and crippling disease of the skin and nerves. The rule for Benedictine monasteries stated that

**27**  *Ilford Hospital Chapel by A.B. Bamford.*

'Care for the sick stands before all', so the nuns at Barking had a clear obligation to provide nursing for the sufferers. Treating leprosy was traditionally the business of Christian missions as the disease was considered a divine punishment for wrongdoing. People were reluctant to touch lepers despite the fact that leprosy is not highly contagious. Ilford Hospital Chapel now has an active and committed group of 'Friends' who organise guided tours, events and activities. The institution is in Ilford town centre but was run by Barking Abbey, reflecting the harmony between these two Essex towns in past times.

King Henry II proved to be a very good friend to the abbey. In 1173 he awarded the foundation a charter of liberties and appointed Mary à Becket, sister of the murdered Archbishop of Canterbury, as abbess. The King had played a very dubious role in the execution

in Canterbury Cathedral three years before. It is possible that Mary gained the position on merit, although her promotion could also have allowed the King to show remorse; certainly Thomas à Becket was canonised in record time. During Mary's time as abbess the leper hospital at Ilford was rededicated to her late brother, St Thomas, in 1175 and Barking Abbey acquired the relics of the saint. This must have afforded her some satisfaction. Very soon after, however, she died and was replaced by Maud, one of Henry II's many illegitimate offspring.

The chapel of St Mary and St Thomas survives today, rather incongruously, in the heart of modern Ilford. It still holds religious services on a regular basis. It consists of a chancel, nave, south aisle, Lady chapel, vestry, north porch, organ chamber and choir vestries. By 1560 the hospital buildings included almshouses, the masters house and lodgings for the priest. This interesting site was excavated in 1959 and 1960. Beneath the original 12th-century foundation some human remains were found, 22 skeletons and three detached skulls arranged in two rows. Some of the bones showed evidence of the individuals having experienced violent deaths. Three spear points were also found in this shallow pit.

Maud's close relationship to the royal family was a great asset. In 1198 her half-brother, King Richard I, forgave the abbess for the debt of 100 marks in cash that she owed the Crown for the revenues from Becontree Hundred. She was not always so fortunate, however, as in 1189 she had been fined for illegally felling timber growing in the royal forest. Maud also offered hospitality to Adgar, a wandering poet who dedicated an abridged version of his French poem, *The miracles of the Virgin*, to the abbess and her nuns.

The final abbess at Barking to be appointed by royal command was Christina of Valognes in 1200. Matters changed in 1213, when Pope Innocent III forced King John to grant the right of free election to all religious establishments in his kingdom. From this time members of the religious order elected their own abbess. King John quarrelled with the Church, and tried to influence the result of the election in September 1214. This required the nuns at Barking to stand absolutely firm, and by September 1215 John was forced to accede to the unanimous election of Mabel de Bosham. This was the year John also argued with rebel barons, who had forced him to sign the Magna Carta in June 1215. In the following year he died, leaving a kingdom divided by civil war.

Mabel de Bosham was by now rebuilding the great abbey, and the extension eastwards of the main abbey church was dedicated in 1240. Mabel resigned from the position in

1247, and the next abbess was an illegitimate daughter of the late King John called Maud. King Henry III presented his half-sister with silver vessels for use at Barking. Her five-year reign was unfortunately cut short by her death in 1252.

Christina de Bosham became abbess next, and her six years in the post were difficult. By 1253 Henry III had become involved in an extravagant scheme to secure the kingdom of Sicily for his second son Edmund which was to prove extremely expensive. Barking Abbey agreed to pay 100 marks a year for five years, a tax known as the clerical tenth, to help finance this scheme. It was doomed to fail, and in 1258 the barons took the government out of the King's hands. As a baron, the abbess was ordered to appear in Chester along with an armed band for an expedition against the Welsh. Not surprisingly, Christina resigned the position in 1258.

A clear picture of the wealth of the foundation in property holdings at this time is provided by the Norwich Taxation. The Barking nuns were patrons of the previously mentioned church of All Hallows-by-the-Tower in London and from this institution they took a pension of half a mark each year. Originally, Barking Abbey had the right to appoint the clergy to the living at All Hallows in Great Tower Street. Following the dissolution, this right was devolved to the Archbishop of Canterbury. They also had a portion of four marks in Fulbourn Church. In the county of Essex they had appropriated four churches and their revenues at Barking, Warley Abbess, Horndon and Dagenham; these churches had a combined income of £108. The nuns were patrons of eight livings worth £35, including Mucking in Essex. The abbess also received 20 shillings a year from the Prior of Dunmow.

**28** *The Curfew Tower or Fire Bell Gate, from the east, in a photograph taken by Caleb Fenn on 28 November 1903.*

**29** *St Margaret's Church and the Curfew Tower surrounded by open space, c.1937.*

**30**   *Church Path around 1900, showing the buildings around the Curfew Tower which were demolished to provide the current open space.*

In 1258 Maud de Leveland was elected as abbess. During this period England was on the brink of civil war, and in June 1260 the abbess was ordered to take arms against bandits. Two months later she was involved in an expedition against the Welsh, followed by similar forays in 1263 and 1264. By now the abbey was in debt and had to sell assets such as timber from the forest. The next abbess, Isabella de Basing, ran into serious expense due to the flooding of her marshes. She too had to sell timber from Hainault Forest and Alderfen Wood to meet her repair costs. It is believed that King Edward I visited

Barking Abbey in March 1294, a mere three months before Isabella's death. Her place was taken by the prioress for less than a year before the election of Anne de Vere in June 1295.

During Anne's reign Barking Abbey featured in the long and disastrous war against the Scots. In November 1306 two men took refuge in the abbey church, probably after claiming sanctuary. One was Hugh Olyfard, a Scottish rebel, who had been removed from the building by June 1307. The abbey also acted as a prison for two high-born wives of Scottish lords, one of whom was Elizabeth, married to Robert the Bruce. In 1308 the Bishop of London forbade wrestling and dancing in the abbey. Anne de Vere died in 1318.

The next abbess was Eleanor de Weston, who was replaced by Yolande de Sutton in 1331. Their reigns, during the years leading up to the Hundred Years' War, are apparently uneventful. The next abbess was Maud de Montagu, one of the younger daughters of William, Lord Montagu. One of her brothers was the Bishop of Ely and another was the Earl of Salisbury. She died in 1352, to be replaced by her younger sister Isabella, who organised for the aisle of St Paul's to be re-roofed. Isabella died in 1358. Her successor was Katherine de Sutton, who is believed to have overseen the construction of the Curfew Tower, or Fire Bell Gate. She also instituted a drama for Easter Day based on the resurrection. The first great floods took place during her time in office. In 1361 land belonging to the abbey in Tolleshunt D'Arcy was flooded. In 1375 the abbess was instructed to pay for the repair of walls on Barking Marsh.

Katherine died in 1377 and Maud Montagu was elected to succeed her. She came to the position during a period of severe financial stricture. Deteriorating weather conditions in the 14th century led to dramatic breaches of marshland belonging to the foundation. Maud was excused from repairing the dykes for one season in August 1377, but a new labour force to repair the sea walls was authorised in March 1380. In July 1380 she was made aware that Barking residents were poaching immature fish in the flooded marsh fields, to the great inconvenience of the City of London. This was owing to the poor state of repair of the river walls, and pressure was put on the abbess to make good the breaches speedily. She protested at this heavy burden. In June 1392, at the Duke

of Gloucester's request, and in consideration of Barking Abbey's considerable losses during the flooding, extensive rights and privileges were granted in Becontree Hundred. In spite of the tragic floods Maud had managed to consolidate and restore some of the privileges of the abbey. She died in 1393 and Sibyl de Felton was elected in her place.

Sibyl was a wealthy widow. During her reign as abbess, however, the damage by flooding became worse. She was given exemption, for ten years, from paying parliamentary taxes as Barking Abbey's income was reduced. Unstable flooded land, such as 600 acres of meadow on Dagenham Marsh, normally used as prime grazing land, was lost. There was a hint of sleaze in 1397, when the running of Ilford Hospital was investigated. It was discovered that the only recent residents had been a chaplain and one poor man, and that the abbess had taken all the issues and profits.

The only surviving service book from Barking Abbey was prepared for Sybil de Felton in 1404. Today it is preserved and kept at Trinity College, Cambridge. It contains some unique hymns created in honour of the Barking saints, including St Erkenwald and St Ethelburga, as specified in the 'Barking Ordinale'.

The next two abbesses ruled for 14 uneventful years. In 1453 Katherine de la Pole, daughter of the 3rd Earl of Suffolk, was elected to take charge at Barking Abbey, where she remained for the next 40 years!

In 1454 the abbess surrendered the right to probate jurisdiction over all laymen who died within the abbey precincts and any abbey servants to the Bishop of London. The convent had jurisdiction only over servants dying inside the abbey who were not married and owned no property or land outside the precincts. In 1457 the prioress and the nuns protested against this ruling, but they were unable to effect any change.

For most of its existence the abbey remained, as it had begun, an aristocratic institution. It widened its horizons a little during the 14th and 15th centuries, when daughters of the wealthy merchant classes, such as Isabel de Basinges, and of county families, such as the Fitzlewes of West Horndon, were finally allowed to join the abbey community. Matters changed radically in the 16th century. The great monastic houses in England and Wales were swept away during the reign of Henry VIII. After the King declared himself Supreme Head of the Church of England all nuns and monks had to take an oath accepting his new status in 1534.

Barking Abbey managed to escape the first wave of suppression in 1536 as its annual income was well above the £200 minimum required to escape dissolution. This only delayed the ultimate fate of the Benedictine community. The abbess Dorothy Barley surrendered the abbey to the King's Commissioner, Dr William Petre, in the Chapter House on 14 November 1539. The Commissioner must have carried out his duties to the satisfaction of the King as he was granted a large parcel of land at Writtle near Chelmsford that formerly belonged to Barking Abbey. In due course his son John was created Baron Petre of Writtle. The Petre family are still prominent in the county of Essex today. Lord Petre owns and manages Ingatestone Hall. The nuns and abbess received a pension following their eviction from the institution, graded according to rank and age. The average pension was five pounds a year. Following the surrender, all the nuns were sent back home within a fortnight!

Accounts of the destruction of the abbey are comprehensive. The Surveyor-General kept extremely detailed records of all proceedings throughout the demolition period, which included tasks undertaken by skilled men such as carpenters and those of unskilled common labourers. Work began in 1541 and was completed in December 1542. The best quality stone was removed to repair the King's manor at Dartford. Lighters from Barking Town Quay transported it. In 1541 lead from the roof was used to repair Greenwich Palace. The pitch and tile hearths used to smelt the lead were discovered by archaeologist Pat Wilkinson in 1972.

*Five*

# AFTER THE DISSOLUTION

After the dissolution the government set up an organisation to dispose of all the monasteries, their properties and estates, called the Court of Augmentations. In Barking the abbey estate continued to function as a single unit known as the Manor of Barking. Having no religious functions, this quickly adapted and became associated with the industrial activities at the watermill standing on Barking Town Quay. North Street Gate became the main entrance to the abbey site while the Curfew Tower became the entrance to St Margaret's parish churchyard from the lower end of East Street, as is still the case today.

**31**  *Barking Church from the River Roding, in a pen and ink drawing by A.B. Bamford, 1894.*

**32** *St Margaret's Church from the north-west.*

**33** *Eastbury House, engraved by W. Watkins after W. Bartlett, 1829. This view shows some agricultural buildings to the south of the property.*

**34** *Map showing Barking and its environs with the Roding flowing south through Barking and into the Thames near Barking Reach, c.1870.*

An agricultural boom followed the dissolution. Some of the new owners of the Manor of Barking lands and property were wealthy London merchants, such as Clement Sysley at Eastbury House. William Pownsett of Loxford pastured all his animals in Barking and grazed his livestock, including 520 sheep and 176 other beasts, on the marshland. The meat from his flock was sold in the butchers' shops of the capital city.

A Victorian copy of a map of central Barking in 1653 made by A.B. Bamford clearly shows the abbey precinct in the form of three fields. The Town Quay and the mill bound the abbey lands to the south-west, where there is a small inlet of water that may have been the site of the abbess's wharf or stairs. On the plan the River Roding appears to be a narrower watercourse than it is at present. A small river ran parallel to the Roding, the Hawkins River,

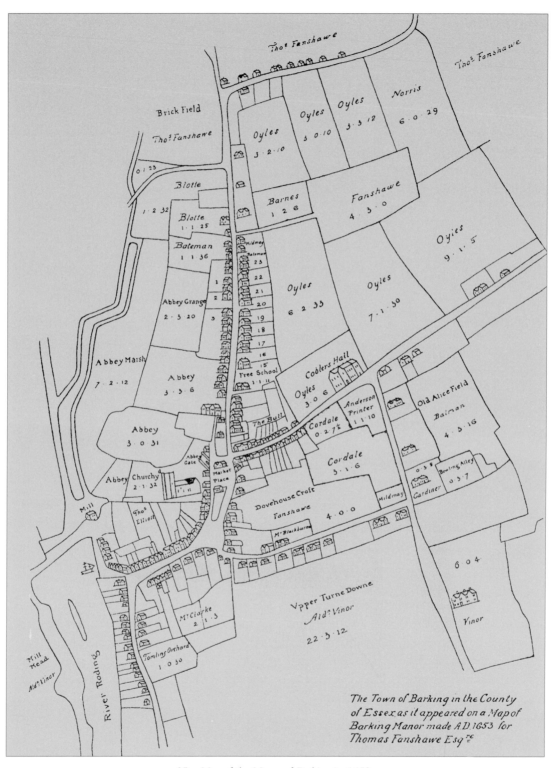

**35**   *Map of the Manor of Barking in 1653.*

on the western boundary of the Abbey Marsh, but this would have changed in the early 1700s when the Roding was dredged and widened between Barking and Ilford towns.

In 1724 the antiquarian Mr Smart Lethieullier, FRS, FSA carried out some excavations on the site of the abbey church. A plan of the site he created at this time reveals the existence of the original precinct wall. It ran along North Street, from the Curfew Tower to an area beyond the current London Road junction. The abbey buildings appear to be enclosed to the south by the churchyard wall, originally the south wall of the abbey church. Depressions here may result from Lethieullier's excavation work or the previous demolition work of 1541.

In 1750, introducing his book *A History of Barking*, Lethieullier wrote,

> Its very Ruins I found were almost Destroy'd, and only a few Stone Walls are traces of the Abby Church and two old Gates remained, to mark the Situation of a Monastery once so famous—both on Account of its Antiquity, Rich Endowment, and the Nobility of the Ladys who thro a long succession had presided over it.

During his excavations, however, Lethieullier only discovered part of the abbey church. The Saints Chapel and an extension to the east remained totally undisturbed. He was able to record the remains of pillars found in the aisles.

In the 19th century the abbey estate was divided when an extension to the London Road was constructed. The southern part of the area was meadow or pasture. Abbey Farm was established in the ruins to manufacture dairy produce. The precinct wall was gradually removed from the 1860s onwards. The site was used by religious organisations in the town for annual Sunday School treats but the ancient monument was not preserved, and further degradation took place after 1881, as North Street Gate became the property of Mr Lodge of Ilford. Mr Frogley recorded that each stone forming the gate was marked, and the entire feature was demolished and transported to Barking Side, where it was recreated in the grounds of Great Gearies house.

In 1910 a new thoroughfare, called Abbey Road, was constructed to join North Street to Fisher Street. This further development detached

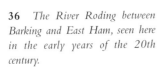

**36** *The River Roding between Barking and East Ham, seen here in the early years of the 20th century.*

the western Abbey Marsh from the ruins. The Vulcan Globe Match Factory was built on marshlands to the west of Abbey Road, and commenced production in 1910 at a time when Barking town was experiencing considerable industrial development. Vulcan, later known as Masters Match Factory, occupied the whole of the western side of the road until the 1960s.

In 1910 Barking Council purchased the abbey site and formulated plans for the ruins to become a public park, providing valuable green space very near the town centre. This provided an ideal opportunity to examine the ruins fully, and the council agreed to undertake archaeological work in partnership with the Morant Club. The task began in January 1911 and took about eight weeks to complete. Only very limited remains of the principal buildings were discovered and the director, Mr Clapham, found the entire dig most disappointing. The designs for the park were abandoned and the newly discovered foundations of the abbey church were laid out as an historic feature. These are in a hollow, well below the original floor level of what was once a huge abbey church.

After the Second World War the abbey site was designated as open space. Housing built in the Victorian and Edwardian periods in North Street and London Road was demolished as slum dwellings, thus clearing much of the nearby land. The open area was extended beside St Margaret's Church to form the Central Area Open Space, which can still be seen in the early 21st century, linking Barking Town Centre to the Town Quay and the River Roding.

In the 1980s and '90s, when Barking Abbey Industrial Estate was built on former abbey land close to the River Roding, Newham Archaeological Service was able to carry out some excavations. Ken McGowan published the results of his dig in 1985-6 when Saxon timber structures were discovered. Features excavated included three Saxon timber wells and a leat, which would have concentrated the water power in the abbey mill. The timbers from the leat were dated by dendrochronology to A.D. 675-730, the early days of Barking Abbey. This indicates industrial activity linked to the development and function of the abbey from the seventh century.

# *Six*

# LORD AND MASTER

Before King Henry VIII closed her foundation down, the abbess at Barking also occupied the position of lord of the manor of Barking. She was a rich and powerful woman in her own right, but owed allegiance to the Crown and could be ordered to take arms on behalf of the King if necessary. She also managed her own demesne estates. Other estates were worked by demesne villeins, unfree tenants who were bound to supply and maintain the religious institution. The Manor of Barking was always the largest and the most valuable of all the assets owned by Barking Abbey. In 1086 it earned almost half the income of the entire institution, and in 1291 more than one third. The estate developed and grew in size during the medieval era. In this period the districts of England had two authorities. The first was religious, embodied by the Church during a period when all held the same benefits, and the second was the secular lord of the manor, whose power was exercised via the manorial court. Strangely, the lord was bound as tightly by manorial custom as any of his humble tenants.

After 1539, the estate became the property of the Crown and King Henry VIII became the lord of the manor. The monarch retained the manorial rights until 1628, when the title was sold to Sir Thomas Fanshawe, the King's faithful steward. The manorial rights on the estate survived until as recent a date as 1926. They involved running the manorial courts, although, unfortunately, most of the proceedings for Barking have completely disappeared.

The Fanshawe family were very influential in the area. Fanshawe Avenue in Barking and Fanshawe Crescent in Dagenham are both named after them. The title passed down the family until Sir Thomas Fanshawe, grandson of the original purchaser, left it to a distant cousin. During his lordship of the manor Sir Thomas was involved in creating two charities to help the poor. The first conveyed the market house and other property to the churchwardens. Rents and profits from these properties were used to support the needy. He also donated five acres of land called 'Cotlands' for the use of the poor in 1679. By 1956 the income from the stock acquired when the land was sold in 1898 was £25 5s. per annum. His will was found to be unlawful and the manor passed to his daughter Susanna. Susanna's daughter, Susan Noel, inherited the estate and sold it in 1717 to Sir William Humphreys, Bt, who died in 1735. William's son, Orlando, left the manor to his two daughters Mary and Ellen, who in turn sold it to the antiquarian Smart Lethieullier, who had excavated at Barking Abbey and already

**37**  *Sir Thomas Fanshawe (1628-1705), lord of the Manor of Barking, pictured with his wife Margaret (1635-74). This painting by Sir Peter Lely is on display at Valence House Museum, Dagenham.*

owned Loxford and Wangey manors in two of Barking's neighbouring parishes. His daughter Mary, who married Sir Edward Hulse, succeeded him and the land descended down the paternal line. Indeed, present-day Hulse Avenue off Longbridge Road in Barking is named after this notable family. In 1847 they owned 1,200 acres of land in the district.

The Manor of Barking was actually formed of many different smaller manors. This book will concentrate on the history of those situated within the bounds of the parish of Barking. The Berengers estate was a free tenement, held of the abbey. This meant that only a small quit rent

was due from the tenants. It was situated to the south of the abbey, in or near Barking town. It became part of the manor of Little Ilford in the 16th century, and played no further part in the story of the manor of Barking.

The Bifrons estate in Barking dates from after the dissolution. John Bamber MD, who died in November 1753, built it up in the early 18th century. He was a wealthy physician of Mincing Lane, London who constructed the 'old mansion' as his country retreat. Bifrons house was situated to the south of Axe Street in the town centre; it had a park, which occupied the area between the current Abbey Road South and Ripple Road. Much of this land was carved out of the more ancient Westbury manor. The next owner was Sir Crisp Gascoyne (1700-61), the Lord Mayor of London. He lived at Bifrons and is buried in Barking parish churchyard.

By 1765 Bamber Gascoyne esquire was based at Bifrons, although as a busy Member of Parliament for several boroughs he spent little time in Barking. His brother Mr Joseph Gascoyne was in almost constant residence on the estate. One of the Gascoyne's immediate neighbours at this time was the seven-year-old Mary Wollstonecraft. Mary's father was employed as the Overseer of the Poor for Ripple Ward in 1767-8 and Joseph Gascoyne was a member of the committee reviewing expenses of the poor and the workhouse. Mary Wollstonecraft's main claim to fame was as a feminist writer. Her first book, entitled *Thoughts on the Education of Daughters*, was published in 1787 but she made her mark with *The Vindication of the Rights of Woman* in 1792, which drew attention to the exploitation and abuse women could suffer when they had no control over their own property or children. She married William Godwin in 1797, and their daughter Mary was born a mere 12 days before her death. Mary also grew up to be a notable author and is best remembered for her gothic novel *Frankenstein*, produced shortly after her marriage to the famous poet Percy Bysshe Shelley.

In 1815-16, Bamber Gascoyne II sold part of the estate to William Glenny and demolished the house. The name 'Bifrons' was later transferred to a large house about a hundred yards east of the original property. The remainder of the estate passed through Bamber II's daughter Frances Mary to her husband the Marquess of Salisbury. Their heir was Robert Gascoyne-Cecil, the 3rd Marquess of Salisbury, who became Prime Minister in

1885. In 1847 he held some 136 acres of land in Barking as well as the Ilford Hospital estate. The rest of the Bifrons estate began to be sold for building development in 1889. (Bamber Gascoigne, the author, publisher and television personality who hosted *University Challenge*, is a descendant of this notable ancestral line.)

The manor known as Dagenham, Dagenhams, Dagenham Place or Jenkins was a free tenement held of the abbey. The manor house stood a mile north of Eastbury House and straddled the border of Barking and Dagenham. The earliest record of this estate dates to before 1273, when the holder Emery de Bezill died. At this time 'Dagenham in Barking' was a dwelling house with outbuildings and land assigned to its use. The land consisted of 101 acres of arable plus 19 acres of meadow. For this plot Bezill paid the abbess of Barking an annual rent of eight shillings and eight pence. Emery's heir was probably one Peter de Besill, recorded in the Feet of Fines for Essex as being paid rent in 1276. Roger de Gildesburgh and John Barnable sold this estate, and others, to John de Northtoft in 1311. In 1326 de Northtoft settled the manor of Dagenham on his son Edmund and his wife. In turn Edmund left the property to his grandchildren Emma and Florence. It is thought that Henry Helion may have married one of these women; he died in 1391 and left land and property, probably including Dagenhams, to his son John.

In 1446 Margaret and Thomas Humphrey and Hugh Lightfoot quitclaimed Dagenham Place to William de la Pole. This formed part of a conveyance of the estate to Robert Osberne. A year later, Osberne was granted free warren in the demesne lands of the manor. Around this time the estate was also being called Jenkins, suggesting the name of a former owner or tenant. It is possible that Simon Jenkyn or

Richard Jenkyn, who held property near Barking Abbey, may also have been tenants on the Dagenhams estate. Robert Osberne leased the estate to William of Waynflete, the Bishop of Winchester, for an annual rent of £13 6s. 8d. in 1448. Two years later Osberne quarrelled with the incumbent abbess of Barking, Katherine de la Pole, about the churchyard key and an alleged violent attack on Katherine and her servants.

By 1456 a grocer called Thomas Plomer held Dagenhams of the abbess at an annual rent of 31s. 2d. plus a ploughshare. Hugh Brown and Henry Wodecock settled the estate on Sir Hugh Brice and his wife in 1479-80; the couple had purchased the adjoining manor of Malmaynes in Barking in 1474. Sir Hugh died in 1496 and left Dagenhams to his young grandson, also named Hugh. He died without issue and was succeeded by Elizabeth, his sister, who married Robert Amadas, Master of the Mint

to King Henry VIII. In 1555 the estate was settled on Elizabeth's granddaughter, who had married Martin Bowes. Frances died in 1556 and within two years her son had sold the manor of Jenkins to Henry Fanshawe, originally of Fanshawe Gate on the borders of Derbyshire and Yorkshire.

This was the start of the Fanshawe family's involvement in the area, which was to last over 400 years. Henry Fanshawe worked as the King's Remembrancer of the Exchequer (a role with similarities to the current Chancellor of the Exchequer) for many years. This made him very wealthy, and he chose to invest his money in land and property. He eventually owned estates in London, Derbyshire and Essex, including the manors of Fulks and Jenkins in Barking. His first wife was Thomasine, widow of Robert Stevens of Rippleside, Barking. She died childless in around 1562 and he married Dorothy Stonard, who

**38** *This engraving of Eastbury Manor House in 1783 by S. Hooper shows both octagonal towers in place. The one to the right was partly demolished in 1814.*

**39** *The north front of Eastbury Manor House, 1823, in a watercolour painting by John Buckler.*

**40** *Eastbury Manor House by A.B. Bamford, 1905.*

41   *The pantry at Eastbury Manor House, Barking. This watercolour painting is by A.B. Bamford, 1907.*

42   *The Servants' Hall at Eastbury House, Barking by A.B. Bamford, 1907. This room is situated on the ground floor of the west wing.*

bore him three daughters. Henry died in 1568 and was buried at St Margaret's Church. Henry had no sons, but made a protégé of his nephew, Thomas, for whom he secured the reversion of the office of Queen's Remembrancer. Before he died, he also conveyed to him the manors of Jenkins and Fulks and the leases of the manor of Clayhall in Ilford and the Ilford leper hospital and its estates.

Thomas Fanshawe (1533-1601) became Member of Parliament for Arundel in 1572 and for Much Wenlock in 1597-8. He married twice, firstly Mary Bouchier and, in 1579, Joan

Smythe. Thomas gained in wealth and purchased the manor of Westbury in Barking in 1571, the freehold of the leper hospital in 1572 and the manor of Ware Park, Hertfordshire in 1576. The eldest son of his first marriage, Henry, succeeded Thomas at work. Queen Elizabeth I described him as 'the best officer of accounts she had and a person of great integrity'. Thomas left the estate to Joan, and after her death in 1622 it reverted to their son, Sir Thomas Fanshawe, who acquired the lordship of the Manor of Barking from the Crown in 1628. Following this, the Jenkins estate descended with the capital manor.

In 1847 Jenkins Farm, later known as Manor Farm, consisted of 345 acres of land managed by a tenant farmer called James Briggs. Agricultural activity continued into the 20th century. When the Becontree Housing Estate was being built in 1937 Jenkins farmhouse was, sadly, demolished to make way for municipal housing.

The only manor house still surviving in Barking parish is Eastbury. The estate is situated about a mile to the east of the town centre and was originally one of the demesne tenements of Barking Abbey. The income from agriculture on the estate, in cash and kind, was used for general housekeeping in the religious foundation. Nowadays 20th-century council houses incongruously surround the Elizabethan gentry house. There was a house of some kind on the site before the dissolution. In 1540 the estate was leased to Nicholas Stodard. In 1545 King Henry VIII granted Eastbury manor to Sir William Denham along with three other local properties. Following Denham's demise in 1548 the manor passed to his daughter, Margery, who was married to William Abbott. This pair sold the estate in 1556 to John Kele, who seems to have been an agent for wealthy merchant Clement Sysley of East Ham, who worked in the City of London. When Sysley acquired the Eastbury estate it was situated in a rural area of farmland, woods and marshes. He had moved to live in Barking parish by 1560. He decided to construct a new home, which was completed by 1574 when Clement referred to it as 'Estbery Hall', reflecting its secular nature.

**43**   *Eastbury Manor House, Barking in 1967, photographed by Egbert E. Smart.*

Timbers in the roof have been analysed by the process of dendrochronology, and they were cut down for use in 1566. This supports the idea that the traditional construction of large Tudor properties took several years to complete.

The Tudor building is an architectural gem. It was constructed on an H-shaped plan with a brick-walled courtyard to the south and an attractive walled garden to the east. The east wing of the house was used by the resident family and the west wing housed all ancillary services provided by domestic servants. The timber skeleton is faced with English Bond red bricks, some parts of which are decorated with diaper work – patterns in grey brick in the shapes of hearts and diamonds. (The suit of clubs would not have been used in a new house as it was considered unlucky.) Much use was also made of moulded bricks, for example in the chimneys. Eastbury House has mullion and transom windows finished with plaster facings painted to resemble stone cladding. The leaded glass panels are filled with very small panes of glass, as the technology did not exist to manufacture large sheets. It is amazing that the Elizabethan Eastbury House has survived without any addition to the original fabric. From the exterior, it must still appear very like the 'dream home' Clement Sysley built in the environs of Barking for his family.

Sysley died in 1578 and left the estate to his wife, Anne, for her life, reverting then to his son Thomas who was a minor. After his death his widow married Augustine Steward. Her second husband had young Thomas Sysley as his ward. The boy, however, turned out to be a real wastrel who was continuously asking his stepfather for money. In view of this difficult family situation, Augustine granted the 500-year lease of Eastbury to his stepbrother, who died around 1629. His two sons then sold the property to William Knightly. In 1649 Knightly's son sold the estate to his mother, Susan. In 1650 she, in turn, sold it to Thomas Vyner, an alderman of London who became a baronet and died in 1665. The manor descended with the family through Sir George Vyner, who died in 1673, and his son Sir Thomas, who died in 1683 without issue.

The Eastbury estate then passed to his nieces, Edith Lambert, Elizabeth Marchant and Elizabeth Tombs. In 1690 all the Vyner family properties in Essex were divided among the heirs and Elizabeth Tombs received Eastbury manor. Her heirs sold it to William Browne in 1714. William Sedgewick, Browne's nephew, sold the manor to John Wedale following his death in 1724. Wedale's daughter, Ann, left Eastbury manor to her cousin Mary, who married the Rev. Wasey Sterry. After his death in 1779 the estate passed to his three sons, but by 1847 the Eastbury bequest only comprised 65 acres of land. Sharing reduced the inheritance as the property descended amongst the Sterry family.

In 1883 Francis Sterry succeeded to part of the estate. He was the rector of Poltimore in Devon and held on to the land in Barking until 1913-14. He then began to sell parcels for building development. Eastbury Manor House had become a virtual ruin by this time, with farm animals occupying ground-floor rooms, and drastic action was urgently needed. It was preserved for posterity only by the enthusiastic actions of heritage organisations. The Society for the Protection of Ancient Buildings campaigned vigorously to raise funds towards the preservation of the Tudor house. The London Survey Committee published a special monograph entitled 'Eastbury Manor House, Barking', illustrated by Hubert V.C. Curtis, in 1917. This encouraged the National Trust to

**44** *Eastbury House courtyard; showing the ruined tower on the extreme right.*

purchase the property, and today it thrives as a centre for the Arts and Heritage. It has attracted major funding for improvements from the Heritage Lottery Fund, offering bright prospects for the remainder of the 21st century.

The manor of Fulkes was located in and near Barking town and was originally a free tenement of Barking Abbey. One Richard fitz Fulk is registered as holding land in Barking in 1203, and the manor is probably named after

**45** *Broadway from North Street, c.1880.*

his family. In the mid-15th century the people who owned Samkynes and Wyfields estates also owned Fulks. Following the dissolution the King granted all this property to his Lord Chancellor, Thomas Audley. It is believed it was eventually acquired by Thomas Fanshawe, and descended along with Dagenhams.

The manor house was located on the east side of North Street, an area that now forms part of the London Road. J.H. Frogley believed the property was used as the parish vicarage until 1794. Fulks manor house became known as Northbury House in the 19th century. James Reed occupied it in 1862. By 1867 the house was supplied with spring water via a well and also had gas laid on. The Quash family, who lived there from 1868 to 1906, then purchased the property. Mr John Quash Senior, a smack owner who had inherited a large sum of money, lived there first followed by his son, John Quash Junior, who died in 1902. The house was demolished in 1936 to make way for the London Road extension.

The manor of Malmaynes was situated in Ripple Side, Barking, adjacent to the Jenkins estate. It was a free tenement of Barking Abbey named after the Malmaynes family who held it from the 13th to the 15th centuries. John and Rose Malmaynes are recorded in the Feet of Fines for Essex in 1316. The estate stayed with the family until around 1460. By 1462 Joan Rigby (*née* Malmaynes) had carried the manor to her husband, John. Joan outlived her spouse, and sold the estate to Sir Hugh Brice in 1474. Until 1555 Malmaynes descended with Dagenhams, which was also owned by Brice. In 1565 Joan Laxton purchased the estate. When she died in 1576 the manor passed to her daughter Anne Lodge, wife of Sir Thomas. It passed to their son William in 1583. The Lodge family sold it to the Fanshawes in 1625, and after this date Malmaynes descended with the capital manor of Barking.

Another free tenement of the abbey was the manor of Porters at Ripple Side, over two miles east of the town centre. It probably

**46**  *Paddock House, Barking.*

**47**   *Great Porters House, in a watercolour by A.B. Bamford, 1903.*

derived its name from the Porter family, who held land in Barking parish in 1220 and 1258. A large estate held by Sir John Norton included the manor of Porters in 1452 and 1456. Sir John and his son granted Porters to Richard Pygot, who died in 1483 leaving it to his son who was a minor. By 1532 Sir Robert Norwich was living at Porters. He died in 1535 and the estate was then held by his widow, Gillian. She passed the property to her relative Humphrey Tyrell, but he sold it to John Lucas. After his death in 1556 the manor passed to his son, Thomas. It descended in the Lucas family until 1630, when Benjamin Ayloffe and Sir Arthur Herris purchased the estate. By 1635 it formed part of the holdings of Thomas Fanshawe, lord of the Manor of Barking, and is believed to have descended with the main estate until *c*.1701.

The manor of Westbury was situated about half a mile to the west of the Eastbury estate. Originally, it was one of the demesne tenements of Barking Abbey. In the period 1321-2 John Yacop was administering 'Westbury and Dagenham' in his position as the abbey's reeve. His records provide a snapshot of the agricultural activity in the area. He describes a well-developed system of mixed farming. Crops sown during this year included oats, rye, wheat, lenten barley, beans and winter barley. The animals reared on the two estates included sheep and pigs, as well as poultry. Most of the sheep appear to have been transported to these farms specially for fattening. The account also records the sale of more than 100 fleeces. The detailed accounts reveal that some milking ewes were housed on the farms, although their produce was not recorded during this season as some of the beasts became diseased and subsequently had to be destroyed.

By the time of the dissolution, the Westbury estate was being leased to Thomas Fuller. In 1545 the King granted the manor of Westbury and other lands to Sir William Denham (a public house in nearby Dagenham Heathway is still named after him). The estate passed to his daughter, Margery, and upon her death to her son, Edward Breame, who died in 1560. His brother and heir, Arthur, sold the manor to Thomas Fanshawe of Dagenhams in 1571. After his death, in 1601, Westbury

was bequeathed to his eldest son, Sir Henry Fanshawe. His son, another Thomas, who later became Viscount Fanshawe, sold the manor to Sir Thomas Vyner in 1649. In the following year he was also able to acquire the Eastbury estate. These two estates descended together until the early 18th century, when part of the Westbury estate was acquired by Sir John Bamber and joined with the manor of Bifrons.

The rest of Westbury manor passed to Blackburn Poulton, who bequeathed it to his son around 1745. His son sold it to Sir Crisp Gascoyne, who retained part of the estate which

**48** *The string orchestra of Westbury Girls School, Barking. The girls are pictured with the cup which they won in the All England Schools Championship in 1914. In the centre of the group, wearing a mortarboard cap and gown, is their conductor, Miss Margaret Coles, headmistress of the school.*

he left to his son, Bamber, who merged this land with the Bifrons estate. Joseph Keeling purchased the small remaining part of the Westbury estate, which included the manor house, from Bamber Gascoyne in 1747. Following the death of Keeling's widow, Alice, in around 1826, Westbury was sold and merged with the estate of Clements in Ilford. A Dr John Manley lived at Westbury House from 1843 to the 1870s. In the 1880s it was offered for sale and subsequently building development began in the area. The old manor house had been demolished before the end of the 19th century.

The name of Westbury still lives on: the Westbury Centre and the *Westbury Arms* are situated on opposite sides of the western section of Ripple Road. The former was originally a large Edwardian school and the latter a public house, now closed. The *Westbury Hotel*, as it was once known, was advertised as the 'best appointed hotel in the town' and could serve customers with 'chops and steaks at the shortest notice'.

# Seven

# WORSHIP AND WITCHCRAFT

A major venue for religious worship in Barking town from at least the 12th century has been St Margaret's parish church. The building was originally constructed within the abbey precincts, and is believed to have functioned as a chapel before being made into a parish church around 1300. It has a complex history, with many alterations and additions taking place right up to the present day. The eastern end of the chancel is the oldest surviving part of the current assemblage, although it is actually a remnant from an earlier church. Many of the major additions to the church, such as the tower, the nave, the inner north aisle, the south aisle and the north and south chancel aisles took place in the 15th century. One wall, explored during building works in 1907, contained an oyster shell inscribed with the date 1501. The churchyard is bounded by the abbey ruins to the north and a ragstone wall to the south, which most probably formed part of the precinct boundary. There is a similar wall in the corner

**49** *St Margaret's Church as it would have appeared from the south-west in 1800, in a watercolour by A.B. Bamford.*

50   *St Margaret's parish church by
A.B. Bamford.*

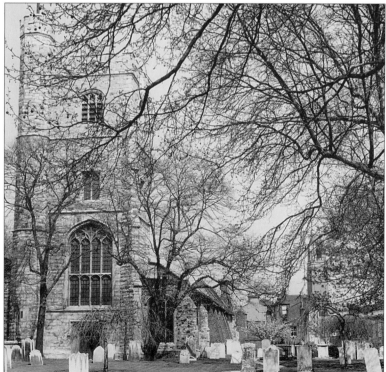

51   *St Margaret's Church and
the parish churchyard by Egbert E.
Smart, 1972.*

**52** *The interior of St Margaret's Church by Clapham. The 'gothic-style' font in the foreground was installed c.1870 and removed in 1928.*

**53** *Procession from the Town Hall to St Margaret's Church for a memorial service for Queen Victoria in January 1901.*

to the north-east of the churchyard. The wall to the west of the churchyard is made of red brick, and is believed to have been erected after the dissolution.

The church is constructed of flint and ragstone rubble and re-uses some old building materials. The lower section of the tower is made from Reigate stone. In 1645 a burial vault was built for the Cambell family to the east of the inner north chapel. It was surmounted by a red-brick chapel which was demolished in 1842. In recent years, this feature has been excavated by Newham Archaeological Service.

The pulpit was constructed in 1727 and originally stood by the central pier in the south arcade. It was moved and lowered in the Victorian era. It currently stands in the nave. There are some impressive brasses and monuments inside the church. On the chancel floor there are three brasses: one depicts a priest wearing academic robes dating from *c.*1480; the second is a palimpsest featuring Thomas and Alice Broke of 1493; and the third, dated 1596, shows John and Elizabeth Tedcastell. Elizabeth died at the age of 43 in October 1596. A space was left to accommodate her husband when he passed on, which happened on 28 March 1612. John was one of the younger Brethren of Trinity House, a member of the Merchant Taylors' Company and a Freeman of the City of London. After 1596 he took a second wife but ordered in his will that he wished to be buried with his first wife in the parish church.

**54** *The view from the tower of St Margaret's parish church, c.1920.*

In a recess of the south wall of the chancel is a carved marble monument to Sir Charles Montagu of Cranbrook dated 1625. In the outer north chapel there is an impressive 18th-century monument to a sea captain, John Bennett, dating from 1706. It features carved ships, motifs which also appear on Captain Bennett's tomb in the churchyard. The outer north aisle has monuments to John Bamber and Sir Crisp Gascoyne. On the north wall of the chancel is a fine marble tablet commemorating the life and illustrious career of Francis Fuller of Beehive and Loxford, who died in 1636. The altar tomb of William Pownsett of Loxford who died *c.*1554 stands in the outer north aisle.

Barking Abbey held the rectories and appointed the vicars. Until the late 14th century two vicars were employed to serve this large parish. One cleric based in the parish church served the northern half, and another dealt with the southern half from the great abbey church. There were also four churchwardens in office, two for Barking ward, one for Ilford ward and one shared by Chadwell and Ripple wards. This role combined lay duties with considerable secular responsibilities. The wardens were selected for office by means of an election and had to take an oath before the local Justices of the Peace. The unit of local government in the area from the late 17th century to the early 20th century was Barking Vestry. The minutes of this organisation, dating from 1694 to 1926, contain a wealth of information regarding local social conditions, and are currently housed in the Archive Department

**55**   *Pupils at the Church of England School, Back Lane in 1897.*

at Valence House, Dagenham. There is also a school run by the Church of England situated next to the ruins of Barking Abbey.

The Vestry operated both as an ecclesiastical and a secular body and usurped many of the powers traditionally carried out by the medieval manorial court. Its heyday was during the 18th and early 19th centuries. Following the final meeting in 1926 some of the active individuals in the vestry, such as Mr W.W. Glenny, became members of the new Barking Urban District Council.

The most important office was that of churchwarden. As well as being the most important lay person in the parish congregation, he also had considerable secular responsibilities. The vicar of the parish church acted in an *ex*

*officio* capacity as Chairman of the Vestry and dealt with much of the important business.

The Church of England has been operating a school in Barking since the mid-17th century when Sir James Cambell bequeathed £667 for the foundation of a free school. The institution was situated in North Street and appears on the map of the town dating from 1653. In 1872 a new school was built in Back Lane, which was enlarged in 1875 and 1889. In 1948 the school was reorganised to educate both infants and juniors and was also granted Aided status. Today the new Church of England School stands on a site adjacent to the Abbey Ruins with an entrance in North Street.

In 1786, much of the responsibility for providing poor relief was transferred by means of the Barking Workhouse Act from Barking Vestry to a new group named the Directors of the Poor. Initially this comprised the six people named in the Act, as well as the vicar of Barking and all Justices of the Peace residing in Barking parish. Any vacancies were filled by co-opting the occupants of properties paying over £200 per annum to the parish. Meetings were held on at least a quarterly basis and the vestry annually appointed four Guardians of the Poor to carry out the requirements of the Act under orders from the Directors. Relationships between these two bodies were generally good. Other appointments included a treasurer, a clerk, other officers and Overseers of the Poor.

The Act required the Directors to fund a workhouse and gave them powers to raise money for this purpose. It also gave them control of all the parish charities raising funds for the benefit of the poor, including the school founded by Sir James Cambell. This state of affairs continued until 1836, when the responsibility for running the workhouse passed to the Romford Poor Law Union. The Cambell School then became part of the Barking National School.

St Margaret's major claim to fame is recorded in the register on 21 December 1762.

**56** *Captain Cook's wedding as seen at the Barking Charter Pageant of 1931.*

**57**   *Barking Vicarage, built in 1794, seen from the garden. This photograph was taken by Egbert E. Smart in 1974.*

On this day the noted explorer and circum-navigator Captain James Cook married a Barking girl, Miss Elizabeth Batts, by special licence. Mrs Cook survived her unfortunate husband, who was killed in Tahiti, by 56 years and the last of her six children by 41 years. She died in Clapham at the grand old age of 93 in 1835. This wedding was to be one of the major scenes from the town's illustrious history selected for use in the Barking Charter Pageant of 1931.

The influential writer on ethics and jurisprudence, Jeremy Bentham, spent most weekends in Barking at the home of his paternal grandmother Rebecca Bentham. According to the local historian James Oxley, her property was situated in North Street, and was sold to George Spurrell following her death around 1761. Spurrell later sold the house to the Directors of the Poor in 1786 in order to construct a new workhouse, and Jeremy Bentham's father was a member of the Workhouse Committee.

The garden of his grandmother's house stimulated a lifelong passion for flora in the young Jeremy. Late in his life he recounted to his biographer, John Bowring, 'So long as I retained my smell a wall-flower was a memento of Barking, and brought youth to my mind.' His autobiographical writings contain accounts of his youth in Barking and of residents such as Mrs White 'who was distinguished for the strength of her jaws, for when considerably above seventy years old, no stone of peach, apricot or nectarine, could resist them'.

Following Jeremy's death, in 1832, his body was bequeathed to University College, London. It was preserved, and is still to be seen on display, dressed in his favourite clothes. Unfortunately, the head deteriorated so badly that it had to be replaced with a wax mask.

The vicars of Barking most probably lodged within the precincts of the abbey in the medieval period. Later, a property in East Street, near the Curfew Tower, was used as a vicarage. This house was let to two tenants in 1683, and was considered to be in need of repair. In his will, dated 1771, Dr Ralph Freeman left £2,000 in trust for repairing or rebuilding the vicarage. The vicar from 1762 to 1780, Christopher Musgrave, spent some of this funding on repairs. His successor, however, decided to obtain statutory powers to construct a new house on a new site and in 1794 a new

vicarage was provided just off Ripple Road. The new building was an attractive, detached, Georgian edifice in grounds with a drive lined with lilac trees. In 1986 Barking and Dagenham Council compulsorily purchased the Barking vicarage from the Church Commissioners. In the 1990s it stood next to the aptly named Vicarage Field shopping centre. In the mid-1990s sympathetically designed office blocks were constructed nearby and the Georgian vicarage became part of the headquarters of the shipping company Cosco UK. The current vicarage is situated further out of the town on Longbridge Road.

As a living belonging to All Souls College in Oxford, St Margaret's has been a stepping

**58**  *Looking north along Ripple Road towards the high-rise flats at the Lintons, constructed in 1962.*

stone to advancement in the Church of England for some vicars, particularly in the 19th century. Herbert Hensley Henson was appointed vicar of Barking in 1888. His superiors hoped that Henson's energy and enthusiasm would help convert people to the Church of England and counteract the influence of the dissenting religions.

His methods worked and he filled the church, his approach appealing particularly to the gas workers at Beckton. He also sat on committees dealing with local education and parish politics. He was not, however, popular with the establishment. In April 1884 he decided to leave Barking in favour of the chaplaincy of Ilford Hospital, a post he held for five years. He progressed to become the Bishop of Hereford, and was the Bishop of Durham from 1920 to 1939. In 1924 he revisited his old haunt to open officially the new public library in Ripple Road. Unfortunately, this building was destroyed by an arsonist in 1967, and many of the original records of the town's history went up in flames.

In the early 1990s St Margaret's Church was extended to provide a vital new Community Centre. This houses a bookshop, refectory, meeting rooms and a crèche. The new building was officially opened on 4 February 1992 by locally born Dr George Carey, then Archbishop of Canterbury. The medieval Curfew Tower still acts as the main gateway to the church and Centre from Barking Town.

Barking has also been marked by various forms of nonconformism, particularly from the 17th century onwards. Around 1658 the Barking Meeting of the Society of Friends, popularly known as the Quakers, was formed. The contemporary practice was for a small congregation to meet in one of the homes of a member but very little is known about the early history of the Barking Friends. In 1672 they purchased a plot of half an acre of land in North Street as a burial ground for members and in the next year paid £87 to acquire part of a Tudor mansion known as Tate's Place, adjacent to the burial ground. The accommodation in the new Meeting House consisted of a Great Hall, two parlours, a staircase and chambers.

Membership of the Society of Friends continued to increase and, in 1691, Barking became one of the monthly sessions of the London and Middlesex Quarterly Meeting, along with other subsidiary meetings at nearby Wanstead, Plaistow and Harold's Hill. In 1703 the Meeting House at Barking suffered storm damage and the repair work was very expensive, but it continued to be used until 1758, when it had to be refronted and partly rebuilt at the cost of £233.

Individual members of the Friends refused to pay parish tithes and church rates. This caused them to be penalised, and details were recorded in special Sufferings Books. One of the more celebrated local examples was that of Richard Claridge (1649-1723), a pamphleteer and schoolmaster. When he refused to pay any rate some of his possessions, including items of furniture, were sequestered and never returned. Claridge felt the Vestry Overseer had persecuted him as Daniel Strange, the man occupying this office, had previously attended meetings of the Barking Friends in the hope of finding a suitable wife amongst the congregation! His quest had not proved successful.

By 1766 the Quakers formed the largest group of religious dissenters active in Barking. After this period, however, the number of members began to decline possibly because of the strict rule forbidding members to marry outside their faith. In 1830 the Meeting House

**59** *The Friends' Meeting House, Barking as depicted by A.B. Bamford in 1905.*

**60** *The Friends' Burial Ground, North Street, Barking.*

**61** *Harvest Thanksgiving at the new Baptist Tabernacle, Linton Road, c.1894. The Rev. Moore and Mr Soul are at the front.*

in Barking closed and the building was not used for sixty years except for special occasions. It opened again in 1891 but the property was assessed as beyond repair by 1908. A new building was constructed which still survives. Since 1971, when the Society of Friends moved next door, this Queen Anne-style structure has been used as a temple by the active Sikh community.

In 1845 Elizabeth Fry was interred in the Quaker burial ground. The remarkable prison reformer was born into the wealthy Gurney family of east London in 1780, and along with her husband and children, she spent holidays at two cottages in neighbouring Dagenham Breach. Mrs Fry was also a minister in the Society of Friends, formally acknowledged and approved by the Barking monthly meeting in March 1811, about a month after the birth of her seventh child.

The Congregational movement also became established in Barking towards the close of the 17th century. Services were held in private rented accommodation from 1782, and a Congregational Church was formed in 1785. A meeting house was constructed on Barking Broadway. This was moved to a site in Upney Lane in 1929, where it still functions today. The earliest known Baptist meetings in Barking were held in hired rooms and private dwellings between 1693 and 1711. The first church, situated in Queen's Road, was not constructed until 1851-2. This property was sold to another nonconformist group known as the Peculiar People (or Peculiars), who were well established in Victorian Essex, in 1898. The Baptists moved to the Tabernacle in Linton Road, which was built in 1893.

Methodism was brought to the town by open-air preachers in the late 18th century. John Wesley himself spoke to gatherings in Barking in February 1783 and January 1784. Meetings were in a wooden hut until a

62    *Central Hall, East Street, c.1935.*

63    *The extension of London Road in 1937 entailed the obliteration of Nelson Street. Looking over to the Central Hall Methodist Church, we gaze across the area occupied by the former manor house of Fulkes.*

**64**  *The* Barge Aground *by Hanslip Fletcher, 1917.*

permanent chapel was built in 1869 on the south side of East Street. This chapel was demolished after the larger Central Hall was constructed in 1928 on the north side of East Street with the capacity to seat 1,500 worshippers. It cost £50,000 to build but was destroyed by enemy action during the Second World War. A new Methodist chapel was erected in Linton Road in 1958. The Salvation Army, founded in 1878 following William Booth's missionary work in the East End of London, opened one of their earliest centres (No. 15) in the Old Bethel at Barking Town Quay in 1873. This moved to the site on Ripple Road in 1922.

New Park Hall still thrives in Barking town centre. This non-denominational religious institution began around 1846, when the Glenny family and associates held meetings in a house in Axe Street. The current hall was constructed in 1931. Today the Glenny name is mostly associated with the branches of a regional estate agent's offices.

In 17th- and 18th-century Barking, the nucleus of the town was the market place. This was situated to the south-east of the abbey and directly to the east of St Margaret's churchyard. In the centre of the market place stood the Market Hall and Court House, which was constructed in 1567-8. The building was paid for by Queen Elizabeth I, lord of the manor at the time. This important edifice contained a hall on the first floor where the manor court was held. Punishment was given locally in the 'cage', containing the stocks, behind a staircase in the court house. The pillory stood in front of the building, and criminal offenders could be humiliated in front of the bustling throng who used the market place.

To the north, south and east sides of the market place were rows of sheds and shops, including the butter market which stood to the south. Early records of a market in Barking date from 1175-9, 1219 and 1456. After the dissolution ownership passed from Barking Abbey to the Crown. In 1616 the market, market place, Market House and some other buildings were conveyed to John Jones, who put them all in trust for the parish of Barking. The corn market was held beneath the open arcades of the Court and Market House. This was where the town's standard bushel was stored. The market bell hung in a bell-cote on the northern end of the building's roof.

The town's fair traditionally took place each year between 22 and 24 October. It was associated with the ancient Feast of St Ethelburga of 12 October. This annual celebration survived right up until 1875. In 1767 Barking was also listed as holding a yearly horse fair on 22 October, which had run from at least the 15th century. Joseph Holmes Frogley described the atmosphere and sights of Barking Fair in his wonderful manuscript history of the town, set down for posterity in the late 19th and early 20th centuries. He noted that the main area for stalls, sideshows and travelling players was the west side of North Street, between *The George* public house and the London Road. Before the late 19th century this was the main thoroughfare. During the Victorian era North Street was sometimes also known as High Street and was the location for a beerhouse aptly called the *Jolly Fishermen*.

Hundreds of donkeys and horses were to be seen all over the town when the fair was operating. Frogley was amused by the sight of Barking fishermen and their wives enjoying donkey rides. Residents could dance to their hearts' content in the booths erected in the grounds of most of the public houses. Two of the well-known characters at these dancing booths were the popular local violinist, Charles Willsmore, and his companion, who was known as 'Blind Scotcher' and played a harp. For three days each year Barking resembled a 'gigantic carnival'. Wombwell's travelling menagerie, founded in 1807, stood on the horsepond beside the Abbey Wall. Visitors could purchase ginger bread and ginger nuts, both of which were considered a culinary speciality of Barking Fair.

There was a much darker side, however, to local life. People were persecuted or even burnt to death for their religious faiths. During the reign of 'Bloody' Queen Mary a lame man from Barking called Hugh Lavercock was burnt to death at Stratford for being a Protestant. The penalty of hanging for witchcraft was introduced by King Henry VIII. It was repealed by Edward VI and restored by Queen Elizabeth I, and during her reign England's greatest persecution of witches

**65** *Barking Court House and Market Hall by Hanslip Fletcher, 1923.*

**66**  *A reconstruction drawing by R.M. Whiston shows the activity around Barking Market Place with the Court House in the centre.*

**67** *(left)   The Elizabethan Court House in Barking, where manorial cases were dealt with, c.1910.*

took place. In 1558 Bishop Jewel delivered a sermon to the Queen noting that, 'Witches and sorcerers within these last few years are marvellously increased in your Grace's realm.'

In August 1579 Elizabeth Harding was charged in Barking with bewitching to death a three-year-old girl and 12 colts. In addition she was charged with causing great injury to Mrs Ellen Goode. She was cleared of the child's death, but found guilty on the other charges. Her sentence was one year in Colchester Prison.

While there, she was charged yet again with murdering the child, found guilty and hanged.

Any woman who looked or behaved strangely went in fear of prosecution. In 1574 Mrs Cecily Glasenbury of Barking (also popularly known as 'Mother Arnold') was sentenced to be hanged as a 'witch and enchantress'. She was accused of causing the deaths of three men and a horse, and of temporarily paralysing a fourth man. She was tried at Brentwood, found guilty and hanged for witchcraft in Barking. Essex was one of the most severe areas for prosecution, the self-styled 'Witchfinder General', Matthew Hopkins, operating in the north-east of the county. The death penalty for witchcraft ceased to be carried out after 1660.

# Eight

# 'SEAFARERS ALL'

Hurrah for Barking's ancient town,
And fishing population:
May ample gains
Reward their pains,
And help enrich the nation.

Verse from *The Song of the Ice* by John Frost, 1849.

It is very difficult today to imagine the Town Quay as the bustling hub of one of the most important Victorian fishing ports in England, but it was, and at its peak, around 1860, the local fishing fleet supplied the avid needs of Billingsgate Fish Market in London. The development of fishing in the area was due to the location on the River Roding. There is mention of a fishery in Domesday Book, most likely a fresh-water enterprise in the river. The close proximity of the rich and powerful abbey, which had been founded in the Saxon era, would have made fish a valuable commodity for the religious community and its supporters.

The first reference to salt-water fishing in the town is in 1320. Several Barking men were prosecuted, along with others from Erith and Plumstead, for the illegal use of nets, popularly known as 'kiddels' and with too fine a mesh, in the River Thames. These nets were destroyed as they were believed to capture small fish and salmon. There was further trouble in 1349, when John de Goldstone of Barking plus

two men from Greenwich were convicted of catching under-sized fish off the east side of London Bridge. Their nets were also ordered to be burnt.

In 1406 the offence was against the inspectors who seized the fishing nets, and were subsequently attacked by a group using bows and arrows – including some fishermen from Barking. This incident caused a riot, and much trouble for the fishermen with the Lord Mayor of London. The abbess's rental of 1456 refers to a 'fish shambles' and there was also a Fish Row. There was most likely a thriving fish market in the town by this time.

The fishing industry began to develop and expand in the 16th century. Timber from nearby Hainault Forest was used to produce ships for the Royal Navy during this era. It was also a time for adventurers on the high seas, such as David Ingram of Barking, who travelled to the Caribbean and West Africa in the 1560s. By the end of the century most of the residents of Barking were involved with

**68 & 69**   *The Page Calnan Wharf on Barking Creek.*

**70**   *Looking south from the Town Quay.*

**71**   *The Town Quay when it used to be a busy industrial area.*

**72** *A frozen mill pond at Barking Town Quay in 1895.*

**73** *Thames sailing barges seen in the ice-bound conditions at Barking in 1895.*

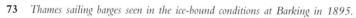

the fishing trade, and the town had become dependent on the industry. In the 17th century most records mentioning fishermen involved them breaking the rules of various authorities. In June 1631 fishermen from Barking had their catches confiscated as they had used trawl nets forbidden by a new government order. The fishermen claimed they had not been aware of the proclamation.

By 1632 there were complaints against Barking men trawling off Whitstable, and the next year a number of them were arrested for trawling illegally. These restrictions in the Thames area seem to have caused the Barking smacks to travel further afield for business. In 1635 a petition was presented to the Lord of the Admiralty by 500 Barking fishermen. They claimed to be obeying the proclamation which

**74**  *The Granary at the Town Quay by Ronald Maddox.*

**75**  *Houses by Barking Town Quay, 1927, which were subsequently demolished.*

**76** *Bracci's Yard, Heath Street, Barking.*

prohibited the use of the trawl, but argued that men from Burnham, Mersea and Whitstable were breaking the law. They requested royal permission to use the trawl, or that other fishermen should be punished for doing so.

From 1642, for 31 years, George Asser and other men from Barking were taking oysters from the River Crouch and the River Roach. These acts defied the Earl of Sussex and his successors, who claimed to have a monopoly in these areas.

Barking smacks were famed for their exceptional speed. Consequently they were used by the Navy as dispatch vessels and privateers. In 1653 a boat from Barking was hired by the Bailiffs of Scarborough to carry a packet out to the generals at sea. In 1655 Vice-Admiral Lawson requested that a vessel from Barking named *Nonsuch*, plus another ketch, should

be armed with six guns and sent to him. In 1656 he hired more Barking smacks, including the *Endeavour* which carried four guns and cost £180 per month, to protect fishermen. A government pinnace called *Henrietta* was stationed at Barking to monitor both smuggling activity and illegal trawls.

During this period press gangs were hired to find new recruits for the Navy. In 1656, 11 ketch men from Barking joined a larger group of fishermen seeking exemption from impressment. Their claim was that they supplied the capital city with lobsters, herrings and mackerel and a petition for their release was presented by the vicar of Barking, the Rev. William Ames. When the Third Dutch War began, in 1672, small vessels and ketches were ordered to assemble at Barking, local men being highly valued for navigational skills acquired in the difficult Thames estuary, which was a mass of treacherous sandbanks.

In 1722 the novelist Daniel Defoe described Barking in his *Tour through Great Britain* as 'a large market town but chiefly inhabited by fishermen, whose smacks ride in the Thames at the mouth of the River Roding'. The fishing industry really began to develop in a big way with the arrival of the Hewett family. Scrymgeour Hewett originally came south, from Cupar in Fife, Scotland, to look after a property owned by his aunt. He believed 18th-century Barking was the most beautiful little village he had ever seen. He settled down, marrying Miss Sarah Whennell, the only daughter of Thomas, a fishing smack owner. Thomas Whennell died in 1837, and the epitaph on his grave in St Margaret's churchyard reads as follows:

> His anchors cast, his nets declined,
> He died in peace with all mankind,
> To heaven above is gone, I trust,
> And there to mingle with the just.

**77**   Above left. *The cutter Don, 1860.*

**78**   Above right. *A Barking Well smack.*

**79**   Right. *Barking trading smack of about 1820-30.*

**80**   *This vessel was originally the* Boy Leslie *of the Short Blue Fleet.*

In 1764 Hewett set up in business with one vessel, the *Liberty*, and financial support from his father, Dr Alexander Hewett. Thus began the Short Blue Fleet in Barking, named after the square house flag flown from the masthead of all Hewett's vessels.

Scrymgeour and Sarah Hewett's second son, Samuel, who was born in 1797, took over the family business. He ran away to sea in 1811 and was later apprenticed as a smack boy. By the time of his father's death, in 1850, Samuel had gained a wealth of practical experience during 14 years as captain of a ship. J.H. Frogley described him as 'a born fisherman'. A number of innovations adopted by Samuel Hewett allowed the fishing industry to boom

in the town in the 19th century. His first major successful idea involved the use of ice as a preservative at sea in around 1840. Barking Well smacks could now travel further into the North Sea, and stay away from land for much longer. Many new people were attracted to work in Barking thanks to the rapid growth of the fishing industry. Their families, squeezed into tenement buildings in and around the narrow streets of the old town, are recorded in the 1851 census returns.

Samuel constructed an ice house in Fisher Street, now known as Abbey Road, and started importing ice from Norway. This proved too costly, so he paid local farmers in Essex to flood their land in winter and collect the ice

81   *Indenture of apprentice William Snow, 1843.*

82   *A page in the 1851 census, detailing Barking fishermen and their wives.*

for storage in his new buildings. Further fishing grounds were explored in, for example, the Dogger Bank. Samuel devised the fleeting system in order to maximise the new opportunities he had created. Fishing vessels remained in the North Sea for between four and eight weeks while a carrier would sail out and collect the daily catch. This would be returned fresh to the London market.

The long journeys away from home and harsh conditions endured on these working trips resulted in the strike of the Barking fishermen, which was reported in the *Illustrated London News* on 30 November 1844. By this time some of the fishermen were spending uninterrupted periods of between three and six months at sea, which they considered to be a huge privation. Their demands to the smack owners were for increased wages and shorter periods of time away.

**83** *The Fisher Street Mission was built in 1878.*

The vessels in the Short Blue Fleet developed into the largest deep-sea fishing fleet in Britain. In 1864 the Hewetts ran the business from Billingsgate, Barking, and Gorleston in Norfolk. The captains of the fishing smacks had a good incentive to maximise the catches as they received a percentage of their takings of fish in addition to their wages. The fleet set out in the early spring each year under the command of an admiral. They would begin catching sole, turbot, haddock and plaice off the Dutch coast. By early May the fishermen would be moving down to Schelling and by mid-July they would end the season off the island of Ameland. Later they would travel into the centre of the North Sea as far as White Water Bank and Botany Gut in order to catch large sole, brill, haddock and plaice. In mid-August the fleet would move to the Dogger Bank for turbot, brill, haddock and plaice. As soon as frosty weather started, good quality sole could be found at the Silver Pits fishing ground.

Mr W. Glenny described the shore visits of the Barking fishermen:

> There were two seasons when every fisherman liked to be ashore; the one occasion was Barking Fair on October 21st or 22nd, the other was ... Christmas. Gingerbread shows, dancing and drinking were the attractions of the former festival whilst good cheer and family meetings distinguished the latter.

Thomas Auckland depicted the colourful heyday of the fishing industry in the town:

> I was never so much in my element as when at Barking among the fishermen and smacks. Those pretty vessels, the *Ranger, Racer, Leander, Ocean Pacific, Blue Bell, Tartar, Saucy Lass, Transit* and a veritable host of others are as fresh in my memory as when they were afloat, and I recall the Barking days of my youth as among the happiest in my life.

There were other young boys, however, who would have less romantic memories of their

**84** Sale notice for Barking smacks.

time at sea. The work in this industry could be extremely harsh and dangerous. In the Victorian period boys as young as 12 were apprenticed to a master and sent to sea. Orphan boys, who were a considerable expense on their local parish, were particularly vulnerable. On 12 March 1836, for example, young William Snow was a pauper of 14 supported by the parish of Barking and apprenticed to one William Spashett. The Hewett family deplored the plight of such apprentice boys, and implored the parishes to take them back in winter to save the poor children from an early grave.

There were cruel masters, however. Thirteen-year-old John Jones lost his life while serving on the Barking smack *Rambler* in 1827. The boy had been lashed to the windlass for six hours and flogged and after this punishment, despite protests from fellow members of the crew, the master had left him tied up with his back exposed to the elements. Entries in the 1861 census provide an insight into the daily living conditions endured by the apprentice boys. James Morgan, the owner of 'Morgan's Fleet' of vessels, is recorded as employing 100 men and 120 boys. He shared his home in Heath Street with his wife and three children, as well as two domestic servants and seven live-in apprentice boys. Eighteen more apprentices were accommodated in the house next door to

**85 & 86** *Robert M. Hewett and the drawing room at Roden Lodge, once home of the Hewett family.*

**87** *The* Barking Smack *public house at Great Yarmouth.*

## NOT SO MANY FISH NOWADAYS.

On account of the unremunerative character of the trawling industry lately, the "Short" Blue fleet belonging to Messrs. Hewett and Co., of Yarmouth, which is the largest fleet of sailing trawlers in the world, comprising as many as 300 vessels, may probably be laid up.

A large number of shore hands have received notice, and fifty vessels are now lying idle in Yarmouth Harbour.

One hundred shore hands have in all been dispensed with at the port, and the detention of fifty vessels at Yarmouth has deprived 300 men and boys of berths.

One cause is the great increase in recent years of steam trawlers, which has depleted the usual fishing grounds of the North Sea.

Messrs. Hewett and Co. have despatched a steamer to Iceland to ascertain whether it is possible for some portion of their fleet to work on the Icelandic coast.

88   *'Not so many fish nowadays'!*

the Morgan family. Around the corner in Fisher Street lived Morgan's younger brother William, another smack owner, who employed 36 men and 40 boys. He lived with his wife, Mary, four domestic servants and an apprentice sailmaker. Following the death of James Morgan in 1865, Samuel Hewett purchased the 29 vessels forming the 'Gamecock Fleet' in 1868.

The spread of the railway network in England was the main reason for the end of the domination of fishing in Barking. It became easier to land fish at east coast locations and transport them to Billingsgate by train. By the close of the 19th century Barking was no longer operating as a fishing port. The decline may have been hastened by a tragic disaster in December 1863, when a gale caused the deaths of some sixty men off the coast of Holland. The Barking smacks were also very expensive to operate, as only small trawls were handled,

and in addition the fishermen did not share in the catch as part of their payment.

In 1865 Robert Hewett, son of Samuel, decided to transfer most of his trawlers to Yarmouth and Gorleston in Norfolk. This was the end of large-scale fishing in the town. A boiler explosion at Hewett's Wharf on the River Roding on 6 January 1899 was the death knell for the industry in Barking. It wrecked the engineering works the Hewett family had built on the east bank of the river. The boiler that burst had originally been used on Hewett's steam trawlers. In 1892 it had been repaired and re-used in the firm's Fisher Street factory. It appeared to function well until 1896, but needed repairing once again in 1897. Following this, it was not used again until the day of the fatal accident.

The blast, which was felt for miles around, caused extensive damage. A large piece of iron

**89** *The rubble and destruction caused by the Barking boiler explosion in 1899.*

**90** *A surviving plate from the ill-fated boiler, engraved with the names of the dead. This artefact is now in the collection at Valence House Museum, Dagenham.*

plate travelled almost a quarter of a mile before entering the home of the Decker family. Ten people lost their lives and several others suffered injuries. The dead included William Page of Barking, whose body was not discovered until four days after the blast as it was buried under a pile of rubble in the fitter's shop where he was blown through a wall.

Funds were raised to support bereaved families like the Humes. Mr Arthur Hume was the organist at St Margaret's Church and his son, also Arthur, apprenticed with the Hewetts, was one of the fatalities. Each widow of a victim was awarded £200 and the injured also received compensation.

After the First World War the Short Blue was rebuilt by the Hewetts, this time at Lowestoft. In 1929 it relocated to Fleetwood, where coal cost less than in Lowestoft. By this time Barking was no longer a fishing port.

# *Nine*

# A NEW TOWN

A fascinating picture of the compact little town of Barking in 1890 was painted by local resident Mr H. Wand:

> Although some development had taken place east of the railway, that side of the town still remained almost wholly under agriculture. Rippleside was a straggling village stretching from the Cemetery to the 'Chequers', and isolated farms and groups of cottages were to be seen along Ripple Road, these being occupied mainly by farm workers. Ripple Road was quite narrow then, bounded on each side by high banks and hedges and overhanging elms. Traffic on the roads beyond the developed area was mainly restricted to the farms, and heavy wagons, laden with market garden produce, left the farms in the evening, and, after a long pause at one of the public houses en route, ambled off to Stratford or Spitalfields.

**91**   *An agricultural Upney Lane in the late Victorian period.*

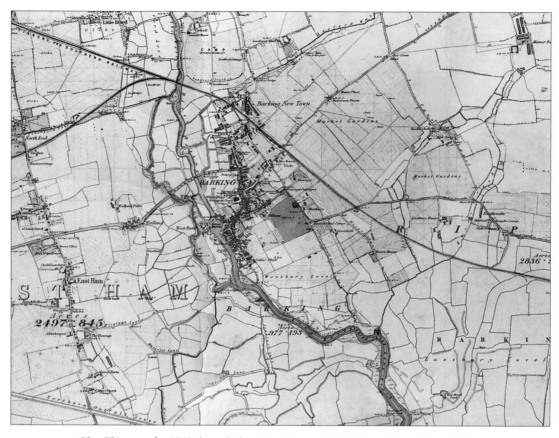

**92**  *This map of c.1860 shows Barking New Town next to fields used for market gardening.*

After the decline of the fishing industry Barking changed significantly in character. The construction of local railway lines radically improved transport links. Many industrial firms were attracted to prime locations near the Thames and the Roding. Houses for workers and commuters were built at 'Barking New Town' on land previously used for agricultural production to the east of the original town centre.

The intensive production of vegetables, fruit and flowers for the London market at Covent Garden took place both in Barking and neighbouring Dagenham in the late 19th century. The largest potato grower in the county of Essex, Mr T. Pittman, operated in this area,

and used horse manure from London which was regularly landed at Barking Town Quay. The dung caused a terrible smell and in 1851 this resulted in a large public outcry over the transportation of manure through the streets of Barking during daylight hours.

The advent of services from London to Tilbury, where new dry docks were constructed in the 1880s, and Southend-on-Sea, which was expanding as a popular Victorian tourist resort, provoked the development of new housing and industries around the major interchange at Barking.

The first main line to cross the ancient parish of Barking was run by the London, Tilbury and Southend Railway. Barking station opened in 1854 when the terminus was located at Tilbury, but two years later the route was extended to Southend. Passengers were now able to travel speedily from Fenchurch Street in the heart of the City out to rural marshlands on the north bank of the Thames estuary. The first station master was William Chalk, who had previously worked in the local fishing industry. He was succeeded by his son, Albert, who was later appointed station master at Southend-on-Sea. His brother, William Chalk, then took over Barking, having previously been station master at Plaistow in East London.

In 1858 a cut-off line opened between Barking and Bow and the Eastern Counties Railway ran a service to Barking via Forest Gate. Between 1885 and 1888 the London, Tilbury and Southend Railway built a direct line from Barking to Pitsea, providing a speedier alternative for visitors to the seaside resort at Southend.

Barking station was rebuilt to handle the ever-increasing volume of custom in 1889. In 1902 the underground District line was extended from Whitechapel to connect with the London, Tilbury and Southend line. The District line was electrified in 1905 and Barking station was altered yet again to accommodate this further development. The acquisition and demolition of property required in order to commence construction began in 1905. About 130 houses and shops were knocked down to make way for the new, enlarged station that opened in December 1907. It had eight platforms and stood to the east of a new goods yard which could be entered via Salisbury Avenue. Displaced residents were offered tenancies in newly built council housing while evicted shopkeepers were compensated for the loss of their premises. The completed scheme was officially opened on 1 April 1908.

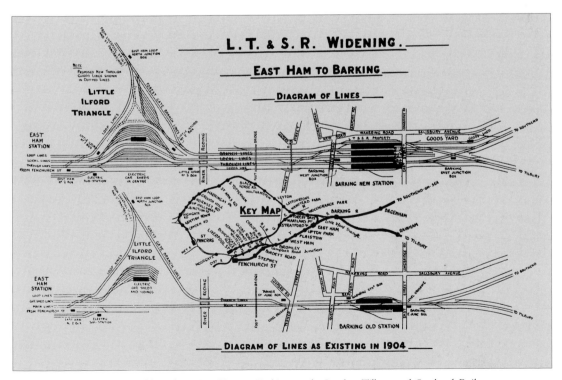

**93** *Diagram of lines from East Ham to Barking on the London, Tilbury and Southend Railway.*

**94**   *Barking railway station, show-ing the up platform and the booking hall, in 1868.*

**95**   *Barking West signal box, which was demolished.*

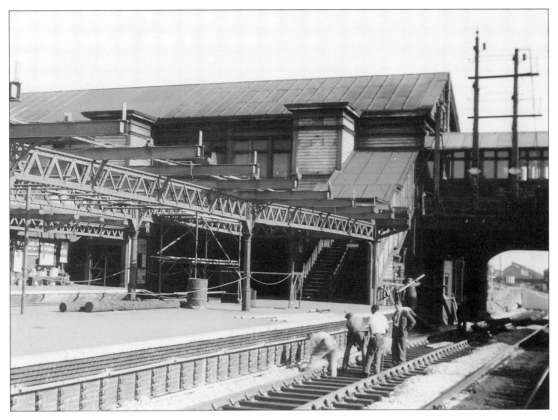

**96** *Mending the track at Barking station.*

By 1910 Barking was the junction at which trains changed from electric to steam traction, and had become an extremely busy station. By 1930 further electrification between Barking and Upminster and new District line stations at Upney, Becontree, Heathway and Dagenham served residents on London County Council's growing Becontree Housing Estate.

Other modes of transport were also developed in the area. Barking Council obtained the necessary powers to run electric trams in 1898, and the line servicing Beckton Gas Works opened on 1 December 1903. The open-top tramcars had a crimson and cream coloured livery and seated 52 passengers. The tram depot was situated in Jenkins Lane very near the gasworks.

Later, other lines were constructed to connect London Road, Barking with the East Ham Tramways line and Fanshawe Avenue with Ilford Tramways via Loxford Bridge. These routes both opened to the public in 1905, radically improving links with neighbouring areas. Some portions of the Barking track were taken over by the London Passenger Transport Board in 1933, and the trams on the Loxford Bridge section were replaced by trolley buses in 1938. In 1940 this also happened on the London Road track. The trolley buses continued until the late 1950s, when running costs became prohibitive and they were discontinued.

A jute-spinning factory was established in Fisher Street (Abbey Road) in 1866 and remained an important presence in the town

**97** *(right)   The frontage of Barking station in 1959, shortly before the radical alterations which took place in the early 1960s.*

**98** *(below)   The concourse of the rebuilt Barking railway station with its concrete-planked roof. With eight platforms, Barking is the largest station on the present-day C2C line.*

**99** *(below right)   The exterior of Barking station in the 1960s.*

until 1891. The Abbey Works was believed to be one of the largest jute factories in England. The buildings were constructed by Thomas Duff on about 12¾ acres of land with an essential frontage on the River Roding. The enterprise prospered until 1886, when foreign competition caused business to decline, and the works closed in 1887, affecting 1,200 factory workers and hundreds of people who worked from home making sacks from the tough material. They reopened in March 1888 but the company was sold to John Ward in the next year. There were several strikes, which resulted in a general lock-out of employees in 1889, and in March 1891 the factory was offered for sale again. The firm finally closed down in April. Religious institutions, such as the Congregational Church, opened relief stations to send home Scottish and Irish employees. The empty factory was purchased in 1896 by Messrs Warne and Company, who employed about one thousand workers to manufacture goods made of rubber.

The marshes at Barking and neighbouring Dagenham were involved in the pioneering days of flight. Frederick Handley Page (1885-1962) established the first aeronautical engineering company in Britain at Creekmouth on 17 June 1909. He leased a corrugated iron shed and a piece of marshland from Samuel Williams and Company Limited. He also acquired flying rights over 2½ miles of rough marshland on the north bank of the Thames between Barking Creek and Dagenham Dock. In 1910 he purchased three sheds belonging to the Royal Aeronautical Society at their experimental flying ground adjacent to Dagenham Dock, and re-erected them at Creekmouth. Part of the marsh near Barking Creek had been built up above the original level by the dumping of clay soil and these sloping dykes were perfect for experimental flights. Handley Page's initial attempts involved a monoplane glider with an undercarriage utilising three bicycle wheels!

During 1910 the first Handley Page powered monoplane was developed, the Type A, popularly known as the 'Bluebird'. A later version of this plane, which had wings and tails varnished yellow, was called 'the Antiseptic' by its pilot, Edward Petre, but was better known at the Creekmouth factory as the 'Yellow Peril'. Early in September 1912 the works moved from Creekmouth to No. 110 Cricklewood Lane, off the Edgware Road between Kilburn and Hendon, in order to expand production. Although the site was advertised for sale as a ready-made aircraft factory, this part of Creekmouth was never used again for that purpose and was later engulfed by Barking power station.

**100**  *In the pioneering days of flight Frederick Handley Page manufactured planes such as this 'Yellow Peril' in a factory at Creekmouth.*

**101**  *Lawes Chemical Company, c.1926. Housing and a school for factory workers and their families can be seen adjacent to the plant.*

Many of the late Victorian enterprises setting up in Barking were involved in the manufacture of chemicals. Sir John Bennet Lawes founded the Lawes Chemical Company Works at Creekmouth in 1857 to make artificial fertilizer and sulphuric acid. Edward Crow's factory produced chemicals at Harts Marshes near Barking Creek from 1862-70. The Barking Guano Works began producing fertilizers at Creekmouth in 1878. William Davey ran a tar distillery at Barking Creek from 1878 to 1906. By the early years of the 20th century Barking had been transformed into a lively industrial centre. In 1930 a huge range of products, including asbestos, matches and clocks, were being made in and around the thriving town.

In 1851 an increasing awareness of health hazards associated with poor housing conditions inspired the creation of the Labouring Classes Housing Act. As the population of the district increased, Barking Urban District Council became a pioneer authority in implementing the Housing of the Working Classes Act of 1890. In addition, the Public Health Act of 1875 forced councils to improve conditions and reduce the amounts of dirt and disease. But it took a serious outbreak of typhoid fever in the late summer of 1896, when eight people died, to make the local authority look seriously at sanitary processes. The new Urban District Council began regularly to inspect and repair the sewers and installed about 500 flushing toilets which dramatically improved conditions in Barking houses. The result of this new policy was an improvement to many existing dwellings and the compulsory closure of others deemed unfit for human inhabitation, over thirty properties being demolished immediately.

At a meeting of the Barking branch of the Social Democratic Federation in 1897,

**102**  *Advert for the Town Quay Steam Wharf and Saw Mills, 1894.*

Barking Council were urged to demolish all slum properties immediately and organise the construction of artisans' dwellings. In the summer of 1897 the Clerk of the Council reported that he had inspected this type of housing in some of England's large cities, such as Birmingham, Manchester and Liverpool. The Surveyor was concerned about the poorer residents in the town not having enough money to pay for better quality housing without taking in lodgers. In his opinion, this was the reason that many working-class people had to live in squalid and cramped conditions in various courts and alleys in the centre of Barking. As land was still available at a reasonable price the Surveyor recommended the construction of two-storey blocks of eight tenements. This proposal was endorsed by the local Medical Officer, who agreed that the cost of rents would mean that ordinary people could not afford to live in new cottages.

Earlier, in 1897, the Medical Officer had reported on adverse conditions he found in various properties in Heath Street, Bifrons Square and Wellington Buildings, all near the centre of town. Common problems were no water supply, shared rubbish disposal, unventilated drains and sewer pipes with joints that were not sealed. All these factors contributed to very poor sanitary conditions.

The medical profession was still greatly challenged by diseases such as smallpox. Barking was hit by an epidemic in 1901–2 which affected virtually all of the county of Essex. The town had experienced no outbreaks of the disease since 1894. By late November 1901 rumours were spread about people being treated in neighbouring Dagenham Smallpox Hospital. Four cases were reported in Barking by the end of 1901 but, luckily, they were all of a mild nature.

**103**   *Bastian's yard, Axe Street before slum clearance took place.*

**104**   *Housing in Barking destined for slum clearance in 1927. This was one of a series of photographs produced by the council to set on record the condition of housing they were trying to eradicate. Specific locations were not named.*

**105**    *Garland's Corner stood at the junction of Ripple Road and East Street. This attractive scene was pictured c.1902.*

**106**    *Blake's Corner, showing the junction of Linton Road and East Street in the 1930s.*

**107**   *This photograph, depicting Jackson's horse-drawn removal wagon, c.1900, shows artisans' dwellings in St Ann's Road which were typical of Barking New Town.*

The procedure to be followed was laid down by the Sanitary Committee. It involved isolating the patient and removing any contacts to a Disinfecting Centre. The house had to be fully sprayed with Formalin, which disinfected the place, and all rooms were fumigated. All articles associated with the patient were removed from the property and disinfected. Smallpox ships were anchored in the River Thames at Long Reach opposite Purfleet, and it was commonly believed the disease originated from them. The Asylums Board was encouraged by Essex County Council to move patients from the ships to a hospital, but during January 1902 the number of cases increased. Five new cases were reported in Barking, one in a house of 18 people. May 1902 was the worst month of the epidemic but in general the situation was improving. On 17 June an inquest was held on Richard Hart who had infected six of his children with the disease. By July the town

was considered to be mainly clear, but it was not until December 1902 that the epidemic was announced as being over. In total, Barking reported 103 cases and there had been 12 deaths.

Artisans' dwellings were built from 1902, when 85 new homes were provided in King Edward's Road. Terraced properties in St Paul's Road, St Margaret's Road and Cobham Road date from 1881 to 1888 and Gascoigne Road was built between 1891 and 1894. All of these dwellings were intended for occupation by local industrial labourers. They provided more hygienic living conditions than the slums in the historic part of the town nearer the River Roding. The 1890 Act was conveniently quoted whenever old properties were judged to be 'so dangerous or injurious to health as to be unfit for human habitation'. Model Cottages in Church Road were demolished in 1901 in order to conform to this legal requirement.

**108**   *H.F. Van built a soft drinks factory on the site formerly occupied by Bifrons House in Barking. He sold out to the famous R. White and Sons in 1890.*

In fact, slum clearance was an urgent priority in Edwardian towns, as councils attempted to improve sanitary conditions. In 1905 numerous families were evicted from Hart Street as their homes were assessed by the local authority as being in a filthy and dangerous condition. The local by-laws had even to be revised to prevent the new municipal houses falling into the same unfortunate state.

The Chairman of the Sanitary Committee officially opened the first block of 14 cottages in May 1901. There had been over 250 applications from prospective tenants for these homes! An article in the *Barking Advertiser* agreed that 'the cottages were much better than many of the tenements in which Barking people are forced to live'. The rooms of these new properties were small, however, and the rents were high. A second block was ready by June 1901, and tenants were selected who could conform to the conditions printed on the reverse of the rent books. By November 1901 the Trades and Labour Council had complained of inferior workmanship in the construction of these new dwellings.

The rents of about seven shillings a week were still considered to be very high. No help was available from the government of the day. In February 1902 the 3rd Marquess of Salisbury (the Prime Minister of the time) was approached to sell some of the land he owned in Barking to provide space to build more double tenements. The Medical Officer of Health was again reporting on conditions unsuitable for housing working-class people; most of the 4,260 houses in Barking were, in his opinion, small and cramped, with poor facilities and expensive to rent.

An insight into the types of residents needing better housing is provided in Dr Fenton's classification of tenants. Firstly he mentions the man earning £2 or more each week: 'he can take care of himself'. The second man earns between 30 shillings and £2: he is required to be both 'honest and thrifty' in order to support his family. In the third category is the man earning below 30 shillings each week who experiences difficulty in paying for good accommodation. The local challenge, according to the doctor, is 'to provide this man with a dwelling with sufficient light and air surrounding it, at a price which enables him to live honestly and decently'. The final class identified by the Medical Officer was the 'casual labourer' living barely above the poverty line. He reported that a purpose-built tenement house under the direct control of the sanitary officer was best for this type of man.

In January 1903 the County Medical Officer visited Barking to view the accommodation provided for labourers. He was most impressed with the dwellings he saw and felt they were better than examples from other districts.

Affairs did not always proceed smoothly. In February 1907 residents of the new houses in King Edward's Road raised a petition to the council requesting a reduction in their weekly rent. This was because landlords of private residences in neighbouring Morley and Howard Roads had reduced the rent from seven shillings to five shillings and sixpence per week. This so outraged the council tenants that ten of the municipal houses were standing empty and more residents planned to leave soon if the council did not agree to their request. On 27 June 1907 the Clerk of the Council, Mr Patmore, wrote to refuse their petition.

Barking acquired numerous rows of small terraced homes, each with a bay window. The population of the district, including Barking Town and Ripple wards, rose dramatically from 5,591 in 1861 to 35,523 by 1921. A new by-pass road had to be created and, in 1909-10, the council built Abbey Road on former abbey lands between Heath Street and London Road. The area needed a 'green lung' and in 1898 Barking Park was officially opened to the general public. Facilities in the park, which occupied some 76 acres of land, included an attractive boating lake, a bandstand and ornamental flowerbeds. Some of these features are still in place today, plus a miniature railway and an indoor bowls centre. On the cultural front, Barking was the first authority in Essex to provide a public library service. Mr Alexander Glenny, of the notable local family, was the first recorded borrower.

The Glenny family have made major contributions to local government, religious life and business affairs in the town, a situation which continues into the 21st century. One of the most distinguished family members was William Wallis Glenny (1839-1933). He lived in Barking and was the first Vice Chairman of Essex County Council, a Justice of the Peace, Chairman of the Romford Board of Guardians and a local historian! More recently, another prominent figure in public life was Kenneth Glenny OBE, JP, a County Alderman from 1951 to 1974.

Edward Glenny managed a Protestant Christian meeting house in Axe Street in 1851. His son, Edward H. Glenny, became founder of the North Africa Nonconformist Mission which ran offices in Linton Road and supervised the training of the missionaries. He established Park Hall and a number of gospel centres around Barking. Edward died in 1925 but New Park Hall was constructed in Axe Street in 1931, charter year. As well as surveying and market gardening, the Glenny family also ran a brewery in Linton Road until 1930, when the concern was taken over by Taylor, Walker and Company, as were 15 public houses.

Improvements in services were also improving the lot of local residents. The first public supply of gas in Great Britain serviced street lights in Pall Mall, London in 1807. The Barking Gas Works was opened in 1839 in Hart Street, now part of Lindsell Road, by Mr Hulett. In 1841 the streets were already lit by gas, but a new firm called the Barking Gas Company was incorporated in 1867, which supplied the town until 1912, when it became part of the Gas Light and Coke Company at Beckton. This was reached by workers on trams which crossed the Roding via the bascule bridge. The council gained powers to

**109**   *The bandstand in Barking Park.*

**110**   *A boat trip on the lake at Barking Park.*

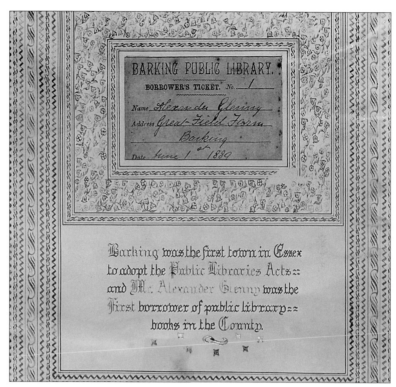

BARKING PUBLIC LIBRARY.

BORROWER'S TICKET. No. *1*

Name *Alexander Glenny*

Address *Great Field Farm*

*Barking*

Date *June 1st 1889*

Barking was the first town in Essex
to adopt the Public Libraries Acts
and Mr. Alexander Glenny was the
first borrower of public library
books in the County.

**111** *The first borrower's ticket for Barking Public Library was issued to Alexander Glenny on 1 June 1889.*

supply electricity in 1897 and a power station was constructed shortly afterwards. In 1927 they contracted out services to the County of London Electric Supply Company, who were already running their own concern at Creekmouth, which became known as Barking Power Station. It developed into one of the major steam generating stations in Europe.

Sanitation proved to be a difficult issue in Barking as the population had risen so quickly during the second half of the 19th century. Health was by now considered to be far worse where water supplies and sewerage systems were poor, and towns were encouraged to produce clean water for residents and improve drainage. In Barking, in 1848, much of the town's sewage still ran along an open drain! Before the 1860s fresh water for drinking was drawn either from a public well situated near the Town Quay or private pumps, or purchased from water carts.

There had been a public enquiry into the problem in 1853, which had no immediate results, but it was not until 1882 that a sewerage scheme was initiated for the town ward. The drainage situation, however, was not finally resolved until the 1930s.

The condition of the water in the Thames was a major concern as it was contaminated by undiluted sewage. In 1868 the vicar of Barking and other local residents sent a petition to the government protesting about discharges of waste from Barking and Crossness sewage stations. The enquiry which followed this complaint exposed Barking as an unpleasant town to live in during the late 1860s. The town's sewerage system was basically an open drain emptying into the basin of the Town Quay. Domestic dwellings were not properly drained, and there were many cesspools. These were reported as being full to the surface and the surrounding subsoil sodden, a veritable breeding ground for all types of disease! The petitioners believed that the river banks, situated near housing, comprised up to ten-feet depth of undiluted sewage from the capital city washing up Barking Creek. An enquiry took place in the Town Hall over six days in June 1869, when all the witnesses failed to persuade the Metropolitan Board of the validity of their case.

A pamphlet published in 1893, entitled 'The process of the Phosphate Sewage Company Limited for disinfecting and utilising the sewage of towns', describes the agricultural techniques being used at Lodge Farm, Barking at the time. Liquid sewage was pumped from the Northern Outfall Sewer through a siphon under the River Roding and distributed from raised troughs over the farmland after being filtered. Such experiments resulted in an epidemic of typhoid fever.

In 1885 a reconstituted Barking Local Board of Health put up a tent on land that belonged to Samuel Glenny for the purposes of treating infectious diseases such as typhoid and diphtheria. The first ward at the Upney Infectious Diseases Hospital was constructed in 1893 at the cost of £5,971. In 1928, a year when infectious diseases were rife in the town, the council adopted a scheme for the erection of a permanent Barking Hospital.

There were better results with plans to provide clean water, and by 1914 only 16 out of the 5,714 houses in the town did not have a supply from the mains. The South Essex Water Works erected a pumping station near the River Roding in 1897, and water was transported from Grays Chalk Quarry to Queen's Road, Barking, where it was reserved for the town's population.

As men returned home to their families at the end of the First World War in 1918, there was a need to provide better housing, or 'homes for heroes'. It was at this time that the largest municipal housing estate in the world was being built. The majority of the Becontree Housing Estate was located in neighbouring Dagenham

**112**   *The new Power House at Barking Power Station, 1925.*

**113**   *The bascule bridge, which was demolished in 1929.*

**114**   *Advertisement for new houses on the Longbridge Estate.*

**115**   *Advertisement for Park Fish Stores on Longbridge Road.*

**116**   *Heath Street Peace Tea, 1918.*

parish, but both Barking and Ilford also had a share of the massive housing stock. By 1939 the number of council house tenants in Barking had risen dramatically to 2,194. This influx of people from slum conditions in cramped East London changed the nature of the area once and for all, from being part of rural Essex into a suburban part of the capital city.

# Ten

# A Charter Mark

That Barking is determined to face the economic difficulties through which our Country is now passing with a progressive policy is clear by the way the Industrial Exhibition and Historical Pageant has been organised by the Borough, and I earnestly express the hope that these days of depression may soon be eclipsed by a restoration of trade and industry in which Barking can take its full share.

HRH Prince George
Buckingham Palace,
22/9/1931.

In the 1920s economic times were very tough in England. A general strike in 1926 involving about three million industrial workers caused great hardship. The Wall Street Crash in October 1929 heralded the Great Depression of the 1930s. In Barking, in 1929, the council was commencing a formal two-year process to investigate a new form of local government for the district at a time of radical change. The Becontree Housing Estate, the largest municipal housing development in the world, was being constructed. This London County Council project covered some 3,000 acres of which 900 were situated in Barking parish. The district had been transformed from a rural and agricultural landscape into a dormitory suburb. In the 1920s the residential part of the town spread eastwards, along Longbridge Road and Ripple Road, filling the spaces between the two. By 1931 the population had increased to 51,270. By the mid-1930s development had stretched to the western edge of the Becontree Housing Estate. In addition, the position of some local boundaries was under review, and Barking was determined to retain its own identity, and not be subsumed into Ilford, Dagenham or a new Becontree division. Action had to be taken swiftly and a strong case for enhanced municipal status presented.

The local council applied for a Charter of Incorporation, which would make Barking a Municipal Borough and afford the town a new status. The first step involved Barking Urban District Council setting a petition before the Lords of the Privy Council for their consideration. This document had to be supported by the signatures of resident householders. The opinion of Barking Council was presented in May 1930 and that of local people at a public meeting in July. The petition was formally lodged in September 1930 and a Public Inquiry was held in the town on 18 February 1931. The Commissioner representing the Lords of the Privy Council was

**117**    *The Public Inquiry of 18 February 1931.*

Mr G. Ewart Rhodes. The inquiry discovered unanimous support from the entire community and the Charter of Incorporation was duly granted by the monarch. This had 'the effect of incorporating all the inhabitants in one under the style of the Mayor'.

This took place against a backdrop of massive worldwide unemployment. In Britain about a fifth of the population were believed to be eating a very poor diet and several hunger marches took place. The town of Barking needed a very good excuse to celebrate, and the 'bringing home' of the Charter provided an ideal opportunity. The Incorporation Committee first met in July 1931 to plan the nature of the celebrations. It was envisaged that all the

residents could be involved in some way. The central event would be a visit to the town by HRH Prince George, who would inaugurate the celebrations and present the Charter on Monday 5 October 1931. All other activities would be arranged to follow this highlight.

Two major strands of the celebrations required a high degree of organisation in a short space of time to achieve success. Firstly, an Industrial Exhibition aimed to encourage manufacturers to establish new factories in the district. Barking was promoted as a good and convenient location for the construction of large industrial units. It was close to the capital city of England, with many vacant sites available at a reasonable cost. In addition, the area enjoyed

**118** *Dress rehearsal for the Charter Pageant in 1931.*

**119** *Prince George's visit to Barking for Charter Day, 1931.*

**120**   *HRH Prince George presenting the Charter of Incorporation to the Charter Mayor, Col A.E. Martin.*

excellent transport links, riverside sites, low power costs and a nearby workforce on the new Becontree Housing Estate. A special temporary exhibition hall measuring approximately 13,000 square feet was constructed in Barking Park. The second major venture was a Historic Pageant, celebrating the rich heritage of the town through twenty centuries. Eleven different scenes were created, plus an epilogue in the form of a grand procession and tableau. The scenes depicted significant events from the town's past, Scene 1 showing 'The Romans at Uphall Camp in AD 43'. This gave various community organisations, such as Barking Bowls Club, and hundreds of individuals the chance to take part in the festivities.

Professionals were engaged to organise and co-ordinate popular town pageants at this time. Frank Lascelles was hired as Master of the Pageant in Barking. Much of the writing was undertaken by pedagogue Col. E.A. Loftus, listed in the *Guinness Book of Records* as the world's longest serving teacher! His father was a master mariner in Hull, Yorkshire, and Ernest was born in 1884. He was educated at Archbishop Holgate's School, York, and began his long teaching career there in 1901. He moved to Essex in 1903 to teach at the Friends' School in Saffron Walden. He had been the first headmaster of Barking Abbey School, founded in 1922, and he researched and wrote extensively about the history of Barking

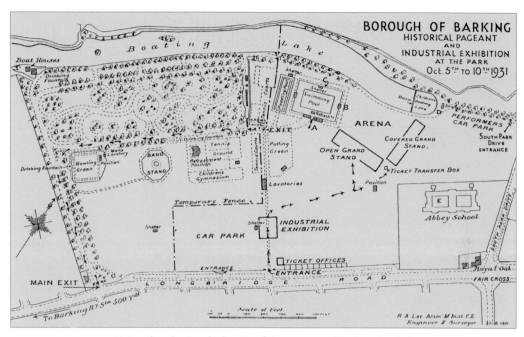

**121** *Plan showing the location of the Pageant and Industrial Exhibition.*

**122** *Barking Park from the air during Charter Week.*

123    *The official opening of the Industrial Exhibition on 5 October 1931.*

124    *Jackson and Company Limited display at the Industrial Exhibition.*

**125** *Anna Neagle, the actress, rows the Charter Mayoress on the lake in Barking Park. They are aboard a rubber dinghy manufactured in Barking!*

**126** *The visit of the Lord Mayor of London to the Charter celebrations on 6 October 1931.*

**127**   *The Mayor of Barking's first banquet, 1934.*

**128 & 129**   *The Procession, 1 October 1931.*

**130** *This char-a-banc outing formed part of the celebrations to mark 'National Baby Week' in 1927.*

Abbey; after his death, at the grand old age of 103, his ashes were scattered on the holy site. Frederick Woodhouse, aided by the British Women's Symphony Orchestra and a host of amateur musicians, directed the musical part of the pageant. Such local gems as 'The Song of Barking' and the Essex May Day Carol were artfully employed.

As well as the main events there was a grand vehicle procession, an Old English fair, tree planting ceremonies, illuminated streets, musical concerts, fireworks displays, a water gala, a souvenir book and special church services, and Barking open-air swimming pool was constructed for local residents. The town has not experienced anything like these magnificent Charter celebrations before or since. Following the events, the town wanted a permanent symbol of its new-found metropolitan status and the council decided to build a new Town Hall. The outbreak of the Second World War in 1939,

## The Song of Barking

Let Barking's ancient glory
Be told in song and story
In long and lasting lays.
With hearts and voices joining
In gladsome songs combining
We sing her deathless praise.

With people in variety
We have a good society
To make us mortals blest:
In social love united
With harmony delighted
We emulate the best.

Our friendship and affinity
Surpasses consangnuinity
As gold surpasses ore;
Success to every brother
Let's stand by one another
Till time shall be no more.

**131**    *The open-air swimming pool in Barking Park, 1934.*

**132**    *The construction of Barking Town Hall.*

**133**   *Shops in Axe Street shortly before demolition in the 1930s.*

**134**  *Bifrons Square, looking north across Axe Street in the 1920s. Shaftesbury Mission Hall is on the left.*

however, meant that the construction of Barking Town Hall had to be put on hold.

The layout of the old town centre changed radically with slum clearances, and large open spaces were created where there had been residential dwellings and shops, such as in Axe Street. Some of the main thoroughfares disappeared entirely, such as Heath Street, and the Town Square and 'Central Area Open Space' were created. It was 1958 before the new Town Hall was officially opened, already looking dated as this brand new edifice still conformed to 1930s design. It dominates the Town Square to this day, due once more for another radical re-design in 2002, its tall clock tower a prominent landmark. This part of East London was also greatly affected by enemy action during the war, particularly in the Blitz. Many areas were available for redevelopment during the post-war period.

*Eleven*

# REGENERATION

By 1939 the banks of the Thames and Roding were occupied mainly by heavy industrial units such as the Cape Asbestos factory. Nearby stood the Becontree Housing Estate. Unfortunately, the Barking area was a sitting target for enemy air raids during the Second World War. Remarkably, industrial production was not seriously affected by damage from the bombing raids. The nearest serious hit was to the Beckton Gas Light and Coke Company's factory on 7 September 1940.

Many local residents volunteered to undertake Civil Defence training in order to help with the war effort. One person who joined the 'Home Guard' was the Assistant Medical Officer in Barking, Dr T.A. Cockburn. One of the incidents he describes is reminiscent of a scene from *Dad's Army*:

**135**  *The Cape Asbestos factory at Barking in the 1930s.*

**136**    *The hall at the rear of Barking Town Hall, now known as the 'Broadway Theatre'.*

**137**    *A Royal Air Force crew at the* Crooked Billet *public house, Creekmouth, c.1940.*

**138**  *Second World War prefabs in Ripple Road.*

One day a demonstration was held in a field and some high brass, including a General, came to see what we were doing. The field had a hill in it and an old car was pushed down it as a target. The whole thing was a fiasco. We found it was not so easy to hit a moving object with a sherry bottle filled with fluid, for the thing is so cumbersome. Most of us missed, and I nearly hit the General who had been unwise enough to stand opposite me. Two bottles did hit the car and they just bounced off unbroken. Obviously, we had to do some more thinking.

Dr Cockburn was renowned for organising excellent entertainments to raise morale during the blackout and the Blitz. Colleagues and local residents were very sorry when he left the area.

The first air raids to affect the Barking district were the armed reconnaissance attacks between June and August 1940. The Battle of Britain and the London Blitz then lasted until about the end of May 1941. From April 1942 to May 1944 the 'Baedeker' raids made much use of incendiary bombs. Finally, in June 1944, the Germans began to launch V1 flying bombs (popularly known as 'Doodlebugs') and V2 rockets. Much of the worst damage to people and property took place in this last phase, which continued until March 1945. The land was left scarred and pitted from the effects of bombing, and much regeneration work was required in the post-war years.

A period of relative stability and prosperity followed the conflict. In the town centre the philosophy of 'out with the old and in with the new' carried over from the major slum clearance projects of the 1930s. The medieval layout of narrow streets, such as Back Lane near St Margaret's, disappeared forever. The actual 'centre' of the town had moved north towards the railway station away from the old hub of the abbey and the parish church. Typical was

**139**   *The demolition of Clarkson Road in the 1960s.*

**140**   *The old* Barge Aground *public house was demolished to create part of the Central Area Open Space.*

**141**   *Demolition of the Court House in July 1923.*

the development of Vicarage Field Shopping Centre in the 1990s. The River Roding and its Mill Pool became detached from the town by the intervening 'Central Area Open Space'. As a result of this, at the beginning of the 21st century there are very few buildings in or near the town centre, except for terraced houses pre-dating 1900. The majority of significant historic properties such as the Court and Market House have been demolished, and Eastbury is the only remaining manor house.

Following the war a new National Health Service and welfare state were established in Britain. Barking already had a hospital, originally set up in 1893 to deal with infectious diseases; this facility was partly rebuilt and enlarged between 1963 and 1966. Barking Hospital was officially reopened by HRH Princess Alexandra on 10 April 1967. It has not, however, survived

more recent restructuring of the local health service and Barking residents now have to travel to neighbouring London boroughs for hospital stays. The large site retains a Minor Injuries Unit and Eye Clinic but the majority of land has been used to provide new private housing.

A large municipal housing development took place to the south of the A13 road between 1954 and 1960 on a piece of former marsh, previously considered to be unsuitable for the construction of housing. The land was reclaimed by means of a system of piles and rafts. It is made up of over 2,000 council houses arranged in a mixture of terraces, apartment blocks, maisonettes, places of worship, schools, library and local shopping centre.

The composition of Barking's population, along with many other areas of East London, has been radically changed by successive waves of

**142**    *The site for the new Barking Hospital in Upney Lane before it was cleared, c.1890.*

**143**    *Construction of the high-rise flats on the Gascoigne estate as seen from Axe Street in the early 1970s.*

**144** *Open space following the demolition of Axe Street.*

post-war immigration. People came initially from former colonies and an Asian community began to thrive in the district. Religious communities are now active in the Sikh Gurdwara (based on the former Friends' Meeting House since 1971) and the new Muslim Mosque in Fanshawe Avenue. Many local businesses, from market stalls to newsagents through to various restaurants in the town, are run by Asians, which adds a cosmopolitan feel to the shopping centre. In

**145** *High-rise flats on the Gascoigne estate and the Town Hall clock tower.*

more recent times people have moved to the Barking area from areas of the world experiencing persecution and conflict. These immigrants, particularly those refugees from the recent Kosovan conflict and from other difficulties in Eastern Europe, have had a major impact upon local services and the existing population.

The proportion of Barking's population made up of various ethnic minorities continues to rise. It is estimated to be about 15 per cent at present. Some of the earlier immigrants are now very well integrated, playing a full part in the development of the area and achieving high status in the community; Barking and Dagenham's first Sikh mayor is Councillor Inder Singh Jamu. There are also community

groups set up to promote cultural diversity, such as the Sunrise Centre for elders from the Afro-Caribbean community based at the New Testament Assembly in Suffolk Road, which aims to provide a sense of belonging for members in a friendly and safe environment. A wide range of activities are organised including story telling, live music and cooking cultural dishes like salt fish and dumpling.

In April 1965 Barking merged with Dagenham. Plans for new building were already drawn up and awaiting action, and in the Barking area slum clearance was still taking place to make way for the proposed housing estates. By the early 1970s work was underway on the Gascoigne estate. This comprised one-,

## Artists' Projects underway within this exciting scheme include:

### Holding Pattern
A collaboration between **Tom de Paor, Graham Ellard** and **Stephen Johnstone**. Holding Pattern creates a visual experience at Lodge Avenue Roundabout for road users, residents and pedestrians alike. A carefully arranged pattern of stainless steel columns is planted on the roundabout, aligning with the various approach roads. Each needle-like column is topped with a small blue light which will create a "cloud" as seen by drivers passing over the roundabout on the flyover.

### Goresbrook Park
**Whitelaw Turkington** (landscape architects) have carried out a consultation exercise to find out the issues and priorities. The next stage involves a design for the park to be undertaken by an artist and landscape architect.

### Goresbrook Junction
This junction marks the eastern end of the Artscape scheme within the borough. A proposal by **Thomas Heatherwick** has been chosen, through an international design competition, to create a fitting end point to the scheme.

### Farr Avenue
An artist/architect collaboration by **Phil Power** and **Jason Cornish**, transforming this previously unwelcoming shopping parade with special paving, planting and lighting. A special sound feature, triggered by a hidden device, will continue to involve, amuse and puzzle the users of the space.

### Subways
Two important pedestrian subways making connections for pedestrians under the A13 have been redesigned by **Anu Patel** and **Pat Kaufman. Anu Patel** proposes a major lighting scheme to create a completely new experience in the tunnel, while **Pat Kaufman** proposes new terraced 'gardens' to give a mediterranean feel.

### Scrattons Farm Housing Estate
**Rayna Nadeem** and artist/architect practice **muf** have worked with the residents of this housing estate to create new surroundings linked to the scale of the residents' own homes and lifestyles. A new park to the south of the estate will include artist-designed benches and bridges and will reclaim waste ground for recreational use.

two- and three-bedroom flats in low- and high-rise developments designed to address housing shortages. Other major developments were the Castle Green and Harts Lane estates.

Recently, however, some of the planning decisions made towards the end of the 20th century have come to haunt the regeneration of Barking. Harts Lane was built on a site previously occupied by the Cape Asbestos Company. People living here have suffered from health problems which resulted in legal cases. In 2002 Mrs Rita Ashworth died after claiming for damage from asbestosis. The continuing construction of housing on former industrial sites, such as at Barking Reach, has caused local residents to question the nature of the land.

They are more aware that the ground beneath their houses may be seriously contaminated with industrial waste.

At the start of the 21st century Barking can be recognised clearly from the air as a patch of blue light. This is the result of 'Holding Pattern', part of the Artworks on the A13, the largest regeneration project involving public art works in England at the present time.

**146**   *A13 Artscape.*

**Light Towers**
The four 36metre interactive light towers are planned to span the length of the scheme creating a straight line that people can use for orientation. Artists **Julie Myers, Gudrun Bielz** and **Jim Buckley** are collaborating with **Tom de Paor** and **Packman Lucas** (engineers). Each tower will incorporate sound and light and will be designed to respond to the local environment.

**The Gallery**
Sited in the main library, a new gallery has been created as a visual arts resource for the whole borough. The gallery hosts exhibitions of artists' proposals for the A13 and other work thematically, changing every 6 to 8 weeks.

**Newlands Park**
A small and run-down park in the south of the borough is being redesigned by **Rob Kesseler** in collaboration with the Council's landscape architects, following consultation carried out by **Community Land Use Ltd.** The designs are being created in consultation with the children and young people on the estate.

**Light Works**
Collaborations with some of the major businesses are currently being explored to develop dramatic projects combining industrial buildings and special lighting effects.

**Special Commissions to Locally Based Arts Organisations**
The A13 Artscape has provided opportunities and funding for new commissions in dance, drama and visual arts involving local arts groups and local people:

- Studio 3 Arts are developing an 'intergenerational trail' which will bring people of all ages together in experiencing and developing arts activities and productions, themed around past and present movements along the road.
- Arc Theatre Ensemble are creating three community plays based on local myths and stories performed at unusual locations.
- East London Dance is producing a series of new dance commissions to take place in sites around the borough, involving the best of British dance makers, working with professional artists and the local community.

# *Bibliography*

Clifford, Tony, *Barking Pubs Past and Present*, London Borough of Barking and Dagenham, 1995

Clifford, Tony, and Lockwood, Herbert Hope, *Mr Frogley's Barking*, Barking and Dagenham Libraries, 2002

Curtis, Susan, *A Guide to Eastbury Manor House*, London Borough of Barking and Dagenham, 1995

Gillespie, Gillian, *Footprints in Time*, London Borough of Barking and Dagenham, 2000

Hill, Alan, *One Hundred Years of Libraries in Barking*, London Borough of Barking and Dagenham, 1989

Home, Dr Robert, *A Township Complete in Itself*, London Borough of Barking and Dagenham

Howson, James, *A Brief History of Barking and Dagenham*, reprinted by Barking and Dagenham Council, 1990

Lockwood, Herbert Hope, *Where was the First Barking Abbey?*, Barking and District Historical Society, 1986

Loftus and Chettle, *Barking Abbey*, 1954

Oxley, J.E. (edited by W.R. Powell), 'Barking and Ilford', *Victoria County History of Essex*, Vol.V, originally published in 1966 for the University of London Institute of Historical Research

# Index

References which relate to illustrations only are given in **bold**.